HANDS-ON ANCIENT PEOPLE
VOLUME II

ART ACTIVITIES ABOUT MINOANS, MYCENAEANS, TROJANS, ANCIENT GREEKS, ETRUSCANS AND ROMANS

The contributions of the Ancient peoples of the Mediterranean, Aegean and Adriatic Sea are monumental influences in Western Civilization today. Consider the architecture of many civic and private buildings, the scientific importance of such objects as the arch and Archimedes wheel; the philosophical advances; and the theatrical, sculptural and artistic legacies. The list is endless. Enjoy adapting intimate artifacts with great and famous objects as you explore the stories of these vital people.

Jim Tilly has designed and perfected all ten books in the Hands-on series.
Not only does he bring excellence to any publication with his graphic talents
but he also stars as a friend and appreciated consultant.

Book design by Art & International Productions, LLC, Anchorage, Alaska
Laurel Casjens took the photographs.
Mary Simpson illustrated the book and assisted with the development of the crafts.
Nancy Mathews and Madlyn Tanner edited and proofread the text.

Books by the author
from KITS Publishing:

Hands-on Africa
(ISBN 0-9643177-7-X)

Hands-on Alaska
(ISBN 0-9643177-3-7)

Hands-on America Vol. I
(ISBN 0-9643177-6-1)

Hands-on Asia
(ISBN 0-9643177-5-3)

Hands-on Celebrations
(ISBN 0-9643177-4-5)

Hands-on Rocky Mountains
(ISBN 0-9643177-2-9)

Hands-on Latin America
(ISBN 0-9643177-1-0)

**Hands-on
Ancient People Vol. I**
(ISBN 0-9643177-8-8)

KITS PUBLISHING
2359 E. Bryan Avenue Salt Lake City, Utah 84108
(801) 582-2517   fax: (801) 582-2540
e-mail - info@hands-on.com web - www.hands-on.com

Thank you to the cooperation of teachers at Dilworth Elementary school in Salt Lake City. The sixth grade students that produced the Etruscan tomb project are **Sara**, **Abhijit**, **Jackson**, **Sarah**, Jayne, **Asena**, Josh, **Ethan**, **Kimmy**, Alma, Max and Randy. Students that are featured on the title page are highlighted. Special thanks to Kathy Johnson and Ron Ricks.
    Students that helped build the Doric Doorway are Randy and Jayne. Students the helped produce the Pompeiian painting are Josh and Max.
    Third grade students from Douglas Elementary School in Granite School District that produced the frieze samples are Heidi, Rachel, Zoe, Alexis, Trent, Will, Josie, Noor, Jenna, Alex, Nicholas, and Scott. A special thank you to Ms. Jueschke.

HANDS-ON ANCIENT PEOPLE

VOLUME II

ART ACTIVITIES ABOUT MINOANS, MYCENAEANS, TROJANS, ANCIENT GREEKS, ETRUSCANS AND ROMANS

Yvonne Y. Merrill

KITS PUBLISHING

TABLE OF CONTENTS

THE SEVEN WONDERS OF THE ANCIENT WORLD

Great feats of engineering and architecture captured the imaginations of people in ancient times. Foremost among these were the famous monuments described by the Ancient Greeks as "The Seven Wonders of the World". All but one of these structures has since been destroyed, so we must rely on written accounts for impressions of how they would have looked.

1. Statue of Zeus at Olympia
This masterpiece in gold and ivory was taken to Constantinople where it was destroyed by fire in 462 A.D.

2. Temple of Artemis at Ephesus
This was a marble temple which was left to decay. Due to the rise of Christianity, this was pulled down in 401 A.D.

3. Mausoleum at Halicarnassus
This grandiose tomb built by King Mausolus of Caria survived until 1522 when the stones were used for a Crusader's castle.

4. Lighthouse (Pharos) at Alexandria
This marble lighthouse was the greatest building in all of Alexandria. It stood until the 14th century A.D. when it was destroyed by earthquakes.

5. Hanging Gardens of Babylon
These beautiful terraced gardens adorned the city of Babylon in the 6th century B.C.

6. Great Pyramid of Giza
Built as a tomb for Egyptian Pharaoh Khufu, this is the *only* wonder that is still standing.

7. Colossus of Rhodes
A huge statue of legendary dimensions straddled the port entry. It was damaged in an earthquake in 226 B.C. and then sold to a Syrian trader.

MAP OF GREEK REGION

20 FEATURED MAP SITES

1. Troy
Trojan horse

2. Lion Gate
Mycenae

3. Knossos, Minoan
Palace on Crete

4. Athens
Parthenon

5. Mt.
Olympus

6.
Thermopolae

7. Temple of
Delphi

8. Tyre
Alexander the Great's
Greatest Battle

9. Rome
Colosseum

5. Mt.
Olympus

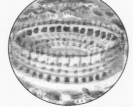

10. Pompeii & Herculaneum
Vesuvius

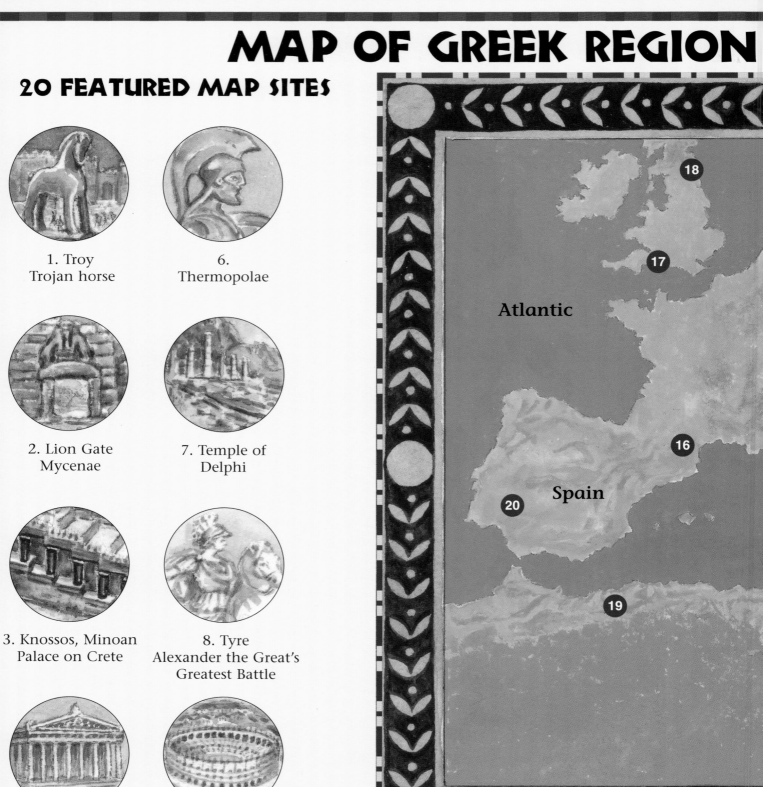

Atlantic

Spain

11. Alexandria
Lighthouse

12. Rhodes
Colossus

AND ROMAN EMPIRE

Black Sea

Turkey

Mediterranean
Sea

20. Spain Merida
Roman Theater

19. Algeria Timigan
Arch & Tower

18. Britain
Hadrian's Wall

17. Britain
Bath

13. Ephesus
Temple of Artemis

14. Tarquinia
Tumuli

15. Cortona
Etruscan Museum

16. France
Pont du Gard Aqueduct

CRETE, MYCENAE AND TROY

The civilization with the greatest influence on the development of the modern world was probably ancient Greece. How do we know about the culture that ended 2000 years ago? The Romans occupied Greece in the 2nd century B.C. and were so impressed by Greek architecture, art and culture that they **copied** what they found. Many of these copies have survived. The Greeks traded throughout the Mediterranean as did the Cretans and Mycenaeans. Sunken ships and excavated sites yielded preserved treasures. Egyptian tombs have contained objects from early Greek craftsmen such as ceramics, figurines and jewelry.

The Bronze Age: From 4000 to 1100 B.C. people found they could make a strong metal by mixing copper and tin. This impacted tools and armaments. People on the Cyclades Islands were carving distinct marble figures of handsome abstracted men and women, animals and birds.

Crete was the largest of the Greek islands and life was centered around many palaces, with the Knossos palace being the most important. Elaborate murals and mosaics which decorated the walls of a complex architecture relate information about an agricultural and sea-trading people who also had the first navy. We know by the giant vessels that palaces stored food and were economic, entertainment and cultural centers as well as

sites of government. The legend of Zeus falling in love with Europa features changing his form into a bull and swimming to Crete with Europa on his back. Their son, Minos, built Knossos and ruled Crete. It is thought that all kings were then named Minos as a royal title. Although there are no written records of the Minoan religious beliefs, their art portrays priestesses and priests conducting ceremonies. One of their most daring entertainments was watching trained acrobats leaping and somersaulting over a bull.

Minoan   scene of bull-leaping   priestess   navy in a mosaic   legendary Minotaur

According to legend, the Athenians paid Crete a tax of seven fit young people. One was Theseus, the son of Athen's ruler. The Minotaur, part bull and part man, was kept in an underground maze. Minos' daughter, Ariadne, fell in love with Theseus and gave him a string to follow his trail through the maze. This trick aided the successful Theseus to return after killing the beast.

The golden age of Minoan culture declined around 1600 B.C. Scientists have discovered that near 1450 B.C. the nearby island of Thera was destroyed by a massive volcanic eruption. Findings indicate that the Minoan way of life was chaotic at this time and palaces were leveled. Though the Minoans attempted to revive and salvage their island, they were weak enough to enable the aggressive Mycenaeans to invade.

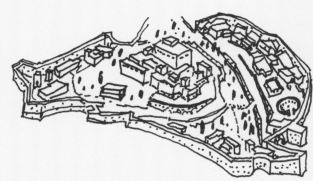

The Mycenaeans were named after their city Mycenae on the mainland of Greece. They lived in small kingdoms with each one based around a separate city. They were never united but traded together. Their cities were walled with underground reservoirs and had an acropolis where the royal palace was built. The palace was much more than a royal residence. It was a military headquarters and administrative base with studios for craftsmen. The Mycenaeans were warriors as evidenced by their bronze armor, shields, daggers and swords.

Mycenaean tombs, discovered in the 19th century, have given us knowledge of Mycenaean skills and beliefs. Their religion was similar to that of the Minoans with a belief in life after death and chief goddesses. The tombs were beehive shaped, known as *tholos.* Important people were buried with great treasures. Unfortunately, the tombs were easy to break into so few treasures are left.

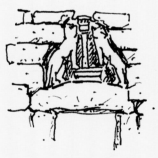

| famous lion gate at Mycenae entry | funeral mask of King Agamemnon | warrior's helmet of boar's tusks | octopus jar |

The Iliad, an epic poem by Homer, tells of a war between Greece and Troy in 250 B.C. The legend is that Helen, a Spartan beauty, was pledged to marry Menelaus, son of Agamemnon, king of Mycenae. Priam, King of Troy, sent his son Paris as part of a delegation to Greece. Paris and Helen fell in love and escaped to Troy. This united the separate Greek kingdoms and together they laid siege to Troy. It was Odysseus who thought of the trick of a giant horse on wheels that would be rolled to the front gate of Troy, appearing as a gift from the Greeks. The famous story is well-known: the hollow horse was filled with Greeks who crept out at night and opened the gates of Troy, ending the siege and destroying the city. Troy overlooked the Hellespont, a waterway that was the entry to Asia Minor from Europe. In 1873 the German archaeologist Schliemann dug through several cities before he found what was ancient Troy.

CENTAURS, STAGS AND BULLS

CENTAURS, STAGS AND BULLS

Materials: Cardboard tubes short and long, strong scissors, masking tape, a variety of brown-toned paints of choice, several large and small-tipped brushes, flour, water and paper strips for papier-mache', accent paint colors.

The Centaur: When early Greek kingdoms fell into the "Dark Ages" from 1100 to 800 B.C., the island of Euboea, near the mainland, continued to prosper. It is here that the half-man figure was made. The vibrant geometric patterns are beautiful. The big ears, heavy brow, and half-smile mark it as an early piece with "personality".

1. Cut a paper towel tube to 7". Cut it halfway through at 3 1/2" so it can bend at the waist. Cut 6 toilet paper tubes in half lengthwise. Cut four of them 3" long and two of them 4" long. Tightly roll each tube and secure with masking tape.

2. Carefully punch holes in the centaur body for the skinny tubes. Insert two 3" tubes in the back for the legs and tape them so they don't move. Next, insert and tape the longer front legs so they won't jiggle. Finally insert and tape the arms. Can the figure stand solidly? Adjust it so it can.

3. Cut the tube to make a jaw line and tape it. With a wad of paper stuck in the open tube top for a skull, tape over the mound. If the figure does not maintain a straight back, tape a 2" strip of cardboard from back to head top. This should strengthen the back.

4. Papier-mache' is done by cutting 1" paper strips about 6"-10" long. Make a paste of 1 c. flour + 1 c. water. Add more water if it is too thick, but *be careful*—it can't be runny. Dip the paper strips into the paste, pressing the paper between your fingers to remove excess paste. Wrap the wet strips around the entire animal. Create the ears, nose and brow with pieces of paper that are covered over carefully. Give the figure a final layer of paper towel strips for evenness (optional). Let it dry overnight.

5. Paint the figure with a wet sponge dipped in a mixed palette of choice. Paint the black designs carefully with a fine-tipped brush.

The Stag:
Using the same technique as described above, the back and neck tube is 10" long, cut at the 5" mark to bend at a right angle. The sloping back legs and straight front legs are 5" long. Now follow the steps as for the Centaur, beginning with a "cut paper tube" in step 1. (continued on page 74)

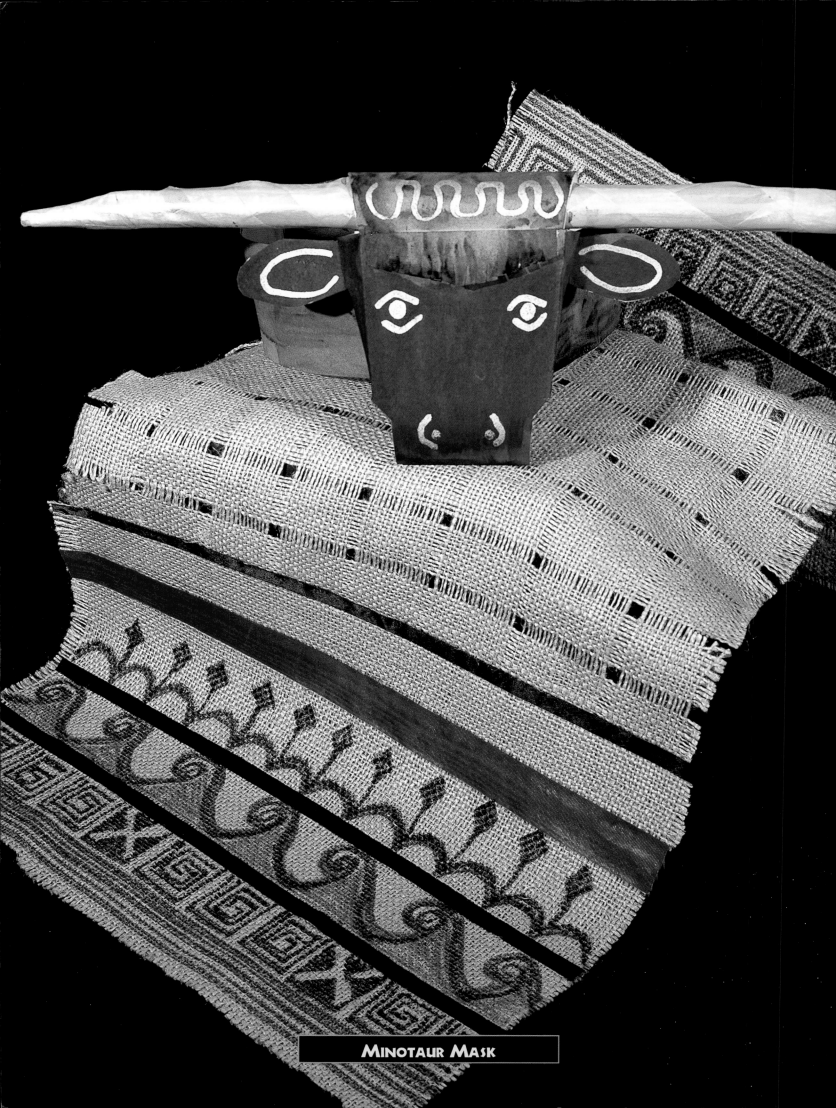

MINOTAUR MASK

MINOTAUR MASK

Materials: Heavy paper 15" x 1 1/2", 9" x 10" construction paper headband, 24" x 2 1/2", masking tape, glue, stapler, scissors, blue paint, gold paint for horns.

1. Enlarge pattern page on 84 by 50%.

2. Lay pattern pieces on construction paper, draw around, and cut out or glue patterns to construction paper and cut out.

3. Color face, ears and forehead fringe. Glue fringe onto bull forehead. Cut ear slots and slide ears into slots. Secure with tape if desired.

4. Roll corrugated cardboard into a tight cylinder, secure with tape, and clip ends to points. Finish wrapping horns with tape. Gild horns with gold paint. Let dry.

5. Fold mask on dotted line and curl nose section under.

6. Center horns inside top section and secure with tape or glue. Snugly roll top section with enclosed horns to back and tape securely.

7. Also on back, match two side pieces to guide corners and staple. Over these, position curled nose section inside its guide corners and staple.

8. Securely attach headband BELOW horns onto back of mask. Measure to individual size and shape.

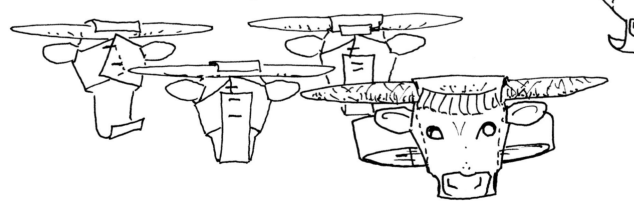

According to legend, an Athenian prince called Theseus went to Crete, where he fought a monster called a Minotaur. It was half-man and half-bull and was kept in an underground maze. In fact, the palace at Knossos had a maze-like design and the king may also have worn a bull's mask in religious ceremonies. Bull-leaping was a daring entertainment, judging from wall paintings. Trained men and women faced the charging bull, grasped its horns and catapulted themselves onto its back.

GREEK VASES

GREEK VASES

Materials: Red air-dry clay, craft sticks for tools, black acrylic paint, medium and small brushes, nail, chalk, planning paper, examples of Greek vases.

1. Choose a traditional vase style from below or create your own unique container. The photograph shows three containers:

2. Greek potters made their fine pots on pottery wheels. Simpler ways to make a pot are with coils or by pinching a pot out of the clay.

Making the pot

3. To make a pinch pot, start with a ball of clay and pinch a hollow in the center. Form your pot by enlarging the opening and smoothing the sides. Add rolled clay coils for handles and a base. If you add a little water to the clay you make "slip" which can be used to "glue" on the handles. When ready, mark the place with a nail, add slip and stick the handle or base to the pot. Let the pot dry. This could take a few days.

4. To build a coiled pot roll several coils the thickness of your finger. Make a flat coiled beginning for the pot base. Smooth the coils together as you stack them. Using a craft stick, smooth the coils inside and outside as you go. This makes a smooth surface for painting and creates a strong pot. Add handles and a base at the end using the "slip" as glue.

Decorating the pot

Greek pottery could have black figures or red figures. Detail lines were scratched out with a sharp point. These defined the designs. Black was painted around the red figures.

1. Draw a paper plan of design for your pot. Holding the pot **very carefully** use chalk to lightly mark the design.
Brush black paint on the figure or around the red figure.

2. When the paint is dry, scratch lines around the figure with a nail point. Be very careful as your pot is fragile and could break.

3. When your work is completely dry, brush off remaining chalk marks.

Much of what we know about ancient Greek life is from pictures painted on red/black vases. In the early Dark Ages vases were painted with zig-zag and geometric patterns. Soon animals and figures were painted between the designs. Egyptian influences of plants and mythical monsters is called the "Oriental" period. The period of Golden Greek culture produced fine vases that portray every aspect of every Greek's life and most aspects of historical events and religion.

MYCENAEAN BOXES

MYCENAEAN BOXES

***Materials:** Any box with a lid, ModPodge or DecoPodge or white school glue that dries clear, many sizes of brushes, acrylic paint, markers of all colors, black fine-tipped marker, water, scissors, white school paper, visuals on early Greek art.*

Round Owl Box: This box is handcrafted. A motif inspired by the owl can be engineered on any size box.

1. Trace around the box lid onto white school paper (or any white paper that is not too heavy and will fit the lid). Add 1/2" as an edge. Age the paper by following the instructions on page 59, part A.

2. On the white paper draw the image, strengthening the pattern with a black marker. Color with any art medium you choose: paint, colored pencils, markers, etc.

3. Cut out the image with the 1/2" edge. Fold down the extra edge and notch with a scissors. Cover the lid and side with brushed-on glue or podge. Carefully center the image and rub from the center to the edges, gently turning over the edge. Let dry when the image is free of wrinkles and bumps and the notched edges are firm.

4. Using more aged paper cut measured strips for the box sides always allowing the 1/2" edge unless it is to frame the lid motif. Our designs are authentic and are from vases, plates, frescoes and ancient fabrics. Refer to the pattern ideas on pages 68 and 69. Draw them first and then color and glue to the prepared box part, carefully applying lid borders.

The bull and octopus are Mycenaean images. The octopus is repeated on many clay forms with wonderful variations in color and tentacles. Ours is especially popular and is painted on a stirrup jar. The patterned bull with the pecking bird is from a mixing bowl. The owl is actually a well-known piece of sculpture in the Louvre art museum in Paris. It is 7th century Corinthian (later than the first two images).

TROJAN HORSE

TROJAN HORSE

Materials: Brown corrugated paper 12" x 24" (available from school supply catalogs or packaging suppliers), cylindrical salt box, 4" x 6" poster board for a supportive base, 17 craft (Popsicle) sticks, glue, tape, scissors, 4 toothpicks.

1. Enlarge patterns from page 72. Patterns are 50% of the actual size. Lay pattern pieces out on flat BACK of corrugated paper and lightly glue. Cut out the cardboard.

2. Flatten the middle of each double leg piece with a stick. Position two sticks in marked places on each end of the double leg pieces. Glue in place. You will have about an inch of unglued stick beyond the dotted lines. These extensions will be slotted into the belly.

3. Only one neck piece is to have sticks glued to it. When those five sticks have dried in place, fold back both shoulders on the dotted line and glue only the head and neck parts together with sticks between. Shoulders will be glued later.

4. Tape four sticks into a fan shape for a tail. Cut tail slot in back circle. Slide in stick tail. Secure on back with tape. The tail circle will be glued to the box later.

5. Position back piece so the metal spout matches tail mark on pattern. Glue back piece in place. Cut leg slots in box as indicated.

6. Attach legs by inserting stick ends into slots. Securely tape flattened middle sections. Cover stick legs with corrugated front and back legs.

7. Remove metal spout and slide fan tail into slot. Glue tail circle in place.

8. Position head and shoulders part on front of box. Glue in place. Turn horse over and glue belly strip in place. Glue together corrugated and regular cardboard for base. Cut four wide slots for legs. Insert legs and raise base about half an inch. Stick toothpick through each wheel and attach to base.

The ***Iliad,*** an epic poem by Homer, tells of a ten-year war between Greece and Troy. The legend is about Helen of Sparta, betrothed to Menelaus, the brother of Agamemnon of Mycenae. Paris, a prince of Troy, fell in love with Helen while on a diplomatic mission to Sparta. Together they escaped to Troy. The Greeks battled around the walls of the strong city. After ten years they left a giant wooden horse outside the gates, ready to be rolled into Troy as a gift. That night the soldiers hidden in the horse emerged and captured Troy.

LA PARISIENNE

A BEAUTY FROM ANCIENT CRETE: LA PARISIENNE

Materials: *Planning paper, nice drawing paper, pencil, crayons or oil pastels.*

About 1500 B.C. on the island of Crete, an artist painted a picture of a beautiful lady. This painting has come to be known as "La Parisienne"–named by the archeologists who discovered her*. Make a portrait of your own in the ancient Cretan style of the side view of a face and front view of an eye.

1. Sketch your idea on planning paper. Tell as much as you can about your subject in a written or verbal presentation.

2. Develop the portrait on nice drawing paper. Color the background with rich detail or in simple colors. Notice her hair, lips, jewelry, and makeup.

*La Parisienne's colored portrait can be found in any quality art book on ancient Crete, Greece, etc. It is recommended that an enlarged color copy be made for students to use as a source of inspiration for their own self-portrait in the Cretan tradition.

Greek Contributions

By 500 B.C Greece was made up of many small independent city-states. Each was called a "polis", hence our ward "politics". They shared the same Greek identity—a common language, culture and religion. Still, they were rivals. Athens, Sparta and Corinth were the most important city-states.

Each polis had a large city, usually walled and built on a hill called an "acropolis" with an open market called the "agora".

Greek society was made up of free men and their families and slaves. Slaves may have lived intimately with the family but were usually not granted their freedom. In Athens free men were divided into two groups: citizens and metics. Citizens were born in Athens and could take part in politics and had to serve in the army and act as officials and jurists. Metics had to serve in the army and pay taxes but could not own property or be involved in politics.

Governing systems evolved with time:

- At first rich landowners ruled, thus an "oligarchy" or "rule by the few". As trade increased a middle class emerged of bankers, craftsmen and merchants. They wanted a say in policies. Conflicts over power occurred and the solution was the emergence of one strong ruler called a "tyrant."
- In 621 B.C. Draco was a severe ruler making terrible laws. Today we refer to a "Draconian measure."
- By 594 B.C. Salon the Reformer ruled with wisdom and justice.
- By 508 B.C. Cleisthenes introduced a radical new system known as a "democracy"—from "demos" the people and "krotos" to rule. Unlike today's democracies only citizens born in the city-state had a say. Women, slaves and even men born outside the city-state were excluded.
- In 429 B.C. Pericles rebuilt the acropolis (destroyed by the Persians) and was the most famous politician in Athenian history.

Athens was the greatest city during the Classical period from 500 to 336 B.C. Athens attracted the best scholars, artists and scientists. According to legend, Poseidon, the god of the seas, fought with Athena, goddess of wisdom and war, over the name of the city. Poseidon promised riches in trade but Athena planted an olive tree. The people decided this was the better gift and named the city Athens. They placed a 40 foot statue of Athena in their temple, the Parthenon. Though it was destroyed, there are many ancient and modern replicas.

The Ancient Greeks developed ideas about art, literature, philosphy, science, politics and history that laid the foundation of European civilization.

Architecture was designed according to strict mathematical principles to give any structure a feeling of balance, simplicity, basic temple design and elegance. The classic building had vertical columns with horizontal beams. The proportions, such as the height and number of columns, were carefully calculated. The columns were decorated with tops called "capitals" which ranged from plain to elaborate:

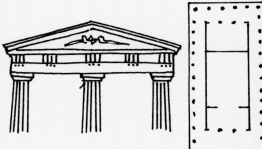

| Doric | Ionic | Aeolic | Corinthian |

The Birth of Literacy: After the Mycenaean Age the art of writing was lost until 800 B.C. The Greeks adopted the Phoenician alphabet with fewer letters and included vowels making it easier to learn and read. The oral legends of heroes and gods was kept alive by "bards", poets who traveled the land, sharing their stories. Homer, the greatest of the bards, wrote the epic poems **The Iliad** and **The Odyssey,** a story of the Trojan war from 850-750 B.C. Herodotus is known as the "father of history". He wrote an account of the Persian war using interviews and accounts of people who experienced the events as his resource material.

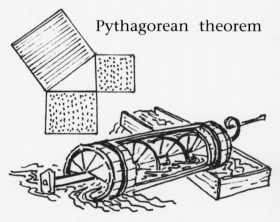

Pythagorean theorem

Archimedes screw

Many basic **mathematical rules** were first thought about and resolved by Greek scholars.
- Pythagoras identified a mathematical pattern in right-angled triangles. He discovered that the square of the longest side (z) of a right-angled triangle is always equal to the sum of the squares of the two sides (x and y). This theorem is taught in schools today.
- Aristotle wrote about biology, zoology, physics, math, astronomy, politics and poetry.
- Archimedes designed a screw-pump to clear water from ships and irrigate fields. Pumps like this are used to irrigate crops in underdeveloped parts of the world today.

Socrates and his student **Plato** were two of the world's greatest philosophers. Socrates believed that it was important to develop a questioning mind. He made his students think carefully about human behavior and examine all things for the truth. Plato recorded his ideas and conclusions.

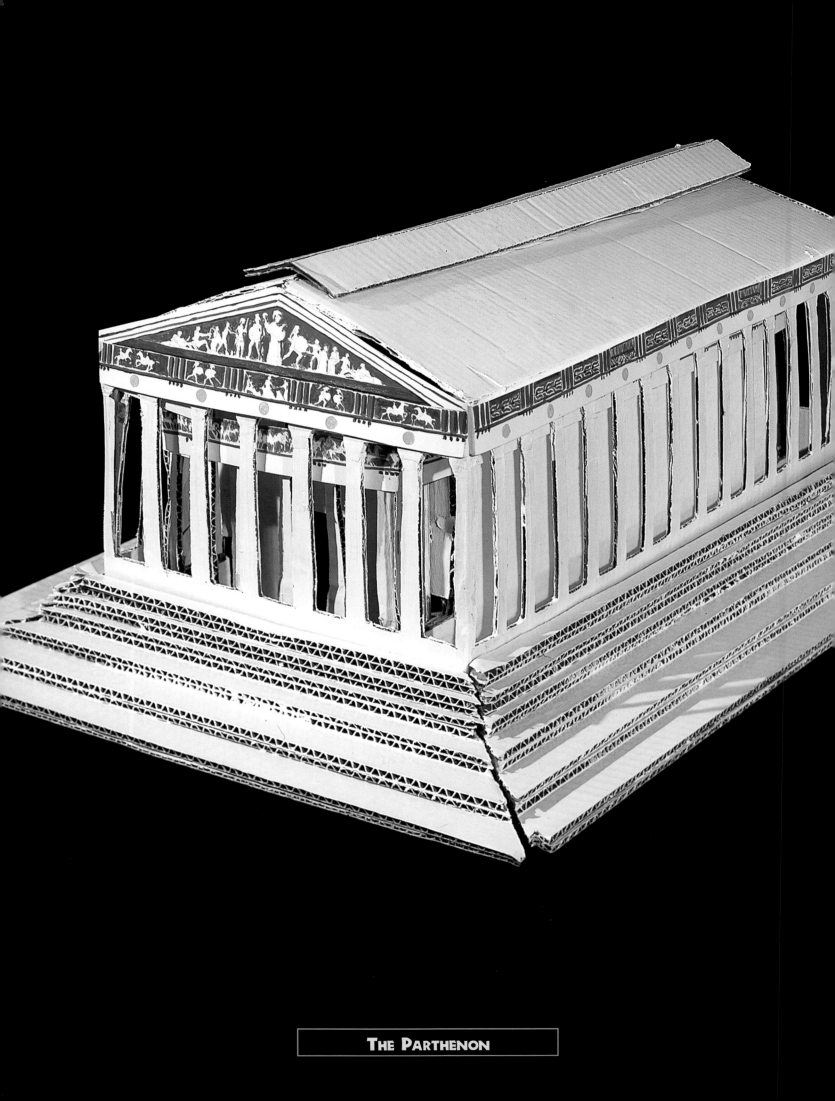

THE PARTHENON

THE PARTHENON

Materials: A box twice as long as wide (two shoe boxes could be combined); ours is a 10" x 21"x 7 1/2" high A-6 envelope box from a printer. A box with flaps provides front and back triangular pediment areas and most of the roof (a box without flaps will have a separate roof so plan on additional cardboard). A smaller, inner box of similar shape, two 6" x 6" and one 6" x 9" pieces of cardboard for partitions, ruler, tape, glue, scissors for light cardboard or exacto knife for heavy cardboard, white paint for marble, optional colors, paint brushes.

(A project for older students or students with careful supervision.)

1. The Parthenon had 8 columns on two sides (see picture on page 73), and 17 columns on two sides which supported a roof. This colonnade surrounded the inner building or *cella* where the 40 foot statue of Athena stood. The *cella* had a six-columned porch at either end. Our floor plan shows some of the magnificent Parthenon design.

2. Calculate the Parthenon proportions. Our *entablature* (triangle pediment, 1 3/4" and horizontal frieze and *architrave,* 1") is 2 3/4" high. The proportional height of our column is one and one half that—about 4" high. The remaining section is for the steps up to the Parthenon. With a pencil mark the triangular point and rooflines. Continue marking the horizontal *entablature* on the long sides. For a box without flaps, draw the triangular pediment on extra cardboard and extend the bottoms so they can be glued onto the horizontal part of your *entablature.)* Measure and mark where the columns will stand. If you are using lightweight cardboard use scissors to cut roof lines and spaces between columns. If using heavy cardboard, have an adult make the cuts for you with an exacto knife.

3. For a box with flaps, the roof is practically complete. All it will need is wide tape or an extra strip of cardboard with a scored center to cover the roofline. Our strip is 2" x 21" long. DO NOT CLOSE THE ROOF YET. If you are making a separate roof, measure the length and width of your box. Add an inch to the width. Cut the cardboard to that size and score the center so it fits your box.

(continued on page 73)

THREE TOYS

ART SCULPTURE

THREE TOYS

Materials: Cardboard, scissors, pattern on page 80, flour, water and strips of newspaper and plain white paper towel for papier-mache', blends of brown, yellow and white paint, small sponge and brush, 2 feet of string and a big-eyed needle, a small balloon, black and brown marker, hole punch, mixing bowl and tool, masking tape, tinfoil.

The Doll

1. Enlarge the pattern on page 80 and cut out the pieces. Trace them on a piece of cardboard and cut them out. There will be five pieces. Carefully punch eight holes, four where the arms and legs attach to the body and four at the top of each arm and leg.
2. In a bowl with a lid mix 1 part flour into 1 part water. When it is the consistency of thick soup and is lump-free it is ready. Tear twenty-five 1" strips of newspaper and ten paper towel strips.
3. Build the face with balls of paper right on the cardboard. Dip your newspaper strips into the paste, running them through your two fingers to remove extra paste. Cover the face ball going over and under the head. Next make a roll for the hair and do the same thing. Next make muscles for the chest and balls for the feet and put paste paper over everything, smooth and unwrinkled. Cover all doll parts with newspaper strips. Put one layer of white paper towel strips over everything.
4. Let the doll dry overnight. Reopen the holes with a sharp tip. Sponge or brush paint the doll with a mixture of earth-colored paint. Tie the arms and legs to the body by punching the needle through the holes.

The Pig

Blow up the balloon. Prepare your paper and paste as you did for the doll. Make the 3" snout of tinfoil and tape it to the balloon. Cut the face shield of ears from cardboard and tape in place. Papier-mache' the pig. Give him a wiggly tail with a twist of paper. Make four feet by cutting a paper tube ends. Let the pig dry. Paint him any color you wish. The ancient pig is made of whitish green clay. You might want to put a slit in his back for a bank.

The Top

1. Cut up the side 3" of a cardboard tube and make a cone. Tape the edges in place.
2. Tape a cardboard circle that fits the top in place. Papier-mache' the entire top. After it has dried, paint it your choice of color. Put the designs on the top and sides with a fine-tipped marker. The ancient top was carved of wood. (continued on page 80)

AMPHORAS

AMPHORAS

Materials: Light-colored railroad board or manila folder, ruler, pencil, plain white paper that is at least 12" x 15", permanent black markers: fine and wide-tipped, or black oil pastels or crayons, scissors, mixed reddish-orange-brown paint, brush and water, paper towel.

Here are examples of the most common vases:

 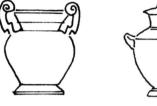 

| amphora | volute krater | hydria | loutrophoros | kantharos | oinochoe |

1. Choose one vase. Draw the shape on a folded piece of plain white paper that is at least the size the vase will be (narrow at the bottom and tall). Look at the pattern page 75 and choose a few patterns. Using a ruler divide the vase into pattern sections and story sections. Look at pictures of vases and the samples in the photograph.

2. Draw the personal story to be told on your amphora: a drawing of a pet, your house and family, friends, sports, etc.

3. Cut out the paper vase from cardboard. Draw the designs with pencil. With black marker, oil pastel or crayon fill in the colors and lines. Work very carefully.

4. Mix the red, orange and brown paint. With a watery brush paint it over the finished vase. Try a corner to make sure it is very watery and the drawings are easily seen. If there is too much paint rub the extra off **carefully** with a wet paper towel.

The Greeks are famous for their painted pottery. We know a lot about Greek life because of the daily, heroic and religious scenes on their containers. In 1000 B.C. designs were geometric. Animals, plants and figures were then added.

Athenian pottery, known as "black-figureware" was sophisticated. From 550-300 B.C. black figures were painted on pots that turned red when they were fired. Spout forms of birds, animals and creatures were cleverly designed on vases.

ATHENA'S OWL PUPPET

ATHENA'S OWL PUPPET

Materials for the Feathered Owl: A piece of poster board or a manila folder 10" x 10", 25 natural colored feathers, pencil, pattern on page 75, strong markers in red, black, brown, 20" string, scissors, 2 brads, several round templates like lids and cups.

Materials for the Paint-Printed Owl: A piece of poster board or a manila folder 7" x 10", potato for cutting shapes to be printed, knife, paper plate for paint palette, brush, water container, 20" string, pencil, scissors, 2 brads, pattern on page 75.

1. Enlarge or reduce the three pattern pieces. Trace around the cardboard and cut out the two wings and owl body.

    a. Design the owl head, wings, body (if feathers are not to be used), etc. Using the cups and lids on both owls create the eye circles (2-3 circles).

    b. For the printed owl cut shapes on the potato and make them "relief" (we cut hearts, triangles and crescents and used carrot tips for the solid circles). Paint the owl parts neutral colors and potato print after paint has dried.

2. After measuring, punch four small holes 1" from the owl wing edge and head to attach wings with brads: two holes in the owl body, two holes in the wing edge.

3. Attach a string across the wing space, tying the string as it secures the edge of each wing. Tie a 14" string at the center of the bridging string. Pull the central string to activate the wings.

The Little Model Magic Owl™

This new sculpting compound worked well for this 4" owl glued on a flat rock. After the owl was molded and dried it was painted. Then it was glued to the rock with school glue and propped against a support overnight until the glue had dried.

The Classical period in ancient Greece was dominated by the city of Athens (500-336 B.C). According to legend, Poseidon, god of the seas, and Athena, goddess of wisdom and war, fought over the naming of the city. Poseidon promised riches but Athena planted a simple olive tree on the Acropolis. It was decided that this was the more valuable gift. The owl was Athena's symbolic animal. Coins in Athens were engraved with owls and the owl became a symbol for Athenians. (see the Roman coin activity on page 57)

THREE MUSICAL INSTRUMENTS

THREE MUSICAL INSTRUMENTS

Turtle Harp

Materials: A plastic container from a roasted chicken, masking tape, 1/4" dowel 15" long, 6 big rubber bands or 100 feet of monofilament, heavy string, 12 small nails and hammer, flour, water and paper strips for papier-mache', black, brown, green, yellow paint and brush, 15" of cardboard.

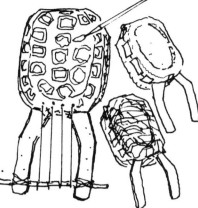

1. Tape the two sections of the plastic container firmly together, inserting the two 15" long cardboard pieces in the container split.
2. Tear newspaper strips, dip in paste (see page 29, part 2 for doll for making paste) and papier-mache' the plastic container and the two cardboard pieces. Dry overnight.
3. Tie on the dowel crossbar. Paint the turtle shell with the turtle pattern (look at a real turtle if possible) and the two cardboard pieces. Hammer in the small nails. Zig-zag the filament for harp strings or stretch the rubber bands. How does it sound?

Timpanon (Tambourine)

Materials: Two 22" x 2 1/2" pieces of light-colored poster board, two sheets of waxed paper cut in a 10" circle, colorful paint, markers or oil pastels, ribbons, stapler.

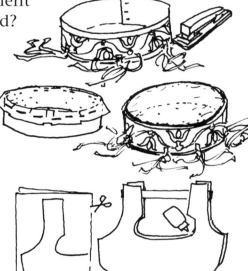

1. Look at pattern page and choose a design for the tambourine. Paint it on the outside strip. Add the colorful ribbon bunches. Staple the ends together.
2. Stretch the waxed paper over the second strip and staple in place (the finished circumference will be around 8"). Slip the second strip with the paper top inside the painted strip. Staple them together. You might add bells, but there is no evidence that the ancient Greek timpanons had bells.

Kithara (similar to a lyre)

Materials: Two pieces 20" x 20" of heavy cardboard, gold paint or marker, 12 small nails, 20-30 ft. of monofilament, brown and black paint, brush, strong scissors, glue.

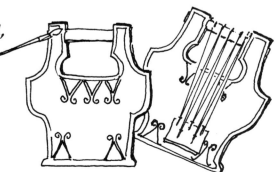

1. Draw the kithara shape on the fold of a newspaper. Cut it out. Trace the shape around the two pieces of heavy cardboard. Cut each out.

(continued on page 74)

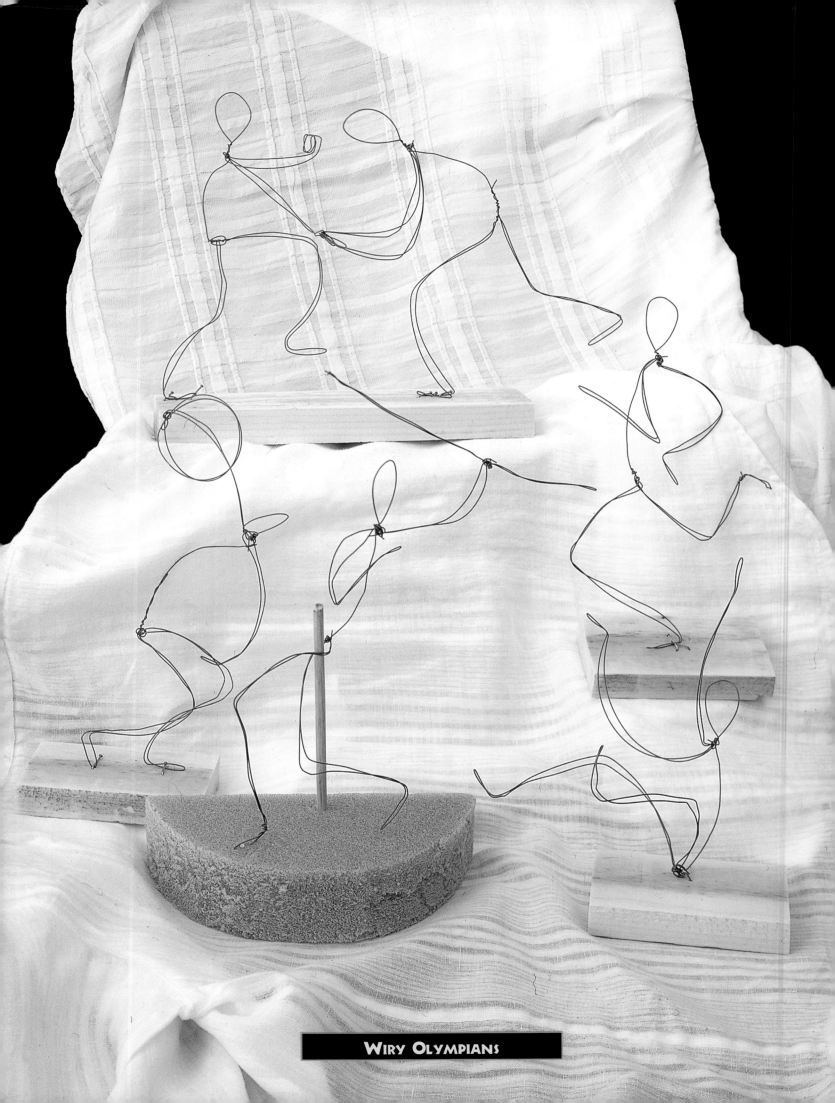

WIRY OLYMPIANS

WIRY OLYMPIANS

Materials: Easily manipulated wire (about 6 ft. for each figure), strong stapler or hammer and small nails, 3" x 5" wood blocks or foam cubes for mounting.

1. Cut approximately 6 feet of wire. Choose the Olympic event from the sample ideas below or research more sports. Make a simple line drawing on paper of the athlete's position. It helps to have a friend pose or use a mirror. Our athlete is competing in the 1500 meter run.

2. Begin the sculpture at the head. Make one or several loops and then twist several times for the neck.

3. Next, extend a length for one arm, double back, wrap around the neck and extend and double back for the second arm. Twist the wire around the neck to secure.

4. Pull wire down for spine and, in what would be the hip area, extend and double back for the first leg. Twist around and extend and double back for the second leg. Secure with several twists at hip and clip off excess wire.

5. Pose the Olympian for the athletic event and mount on the block with a heavy-duty stapler or hammer and small nails.

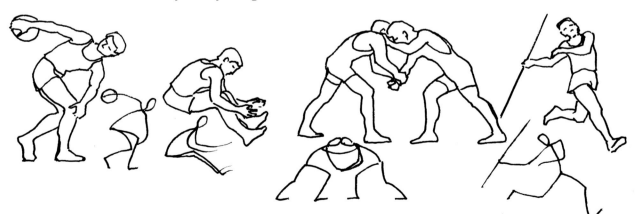

The Olympic games were first held in Greece in 776 B.C. The first games lasted one day and consisted of a single event: a foot race. Later, games lasted a week and featured a variety of races: the javelin throw, discus throw, long jump, boxing, wrestling, chariot racing and other competitions. Women participated separately and were not permitted to view the male competitions as most of the time the athletes were nude.

Doric Doorway

DORIC DOORWAY

Materials: Three 22" x 18" pieces of white poster board, white corrugated paper from roll, white tape, masking tape, glue, scissors, box lids (we used A-6 envelope lids from a printer), optional standard brown cardboard for additional details.

The Doorway

Classic Doric style architecture has three main parts: the stepped platform, the columns, and the entablature which is anything above the columns. We show the stepped platform, the columns topped by square capitals and an entablature with a divided triangular cornice and a horizontal architrave. Measure your classroom doorway. Ours is 80" high.
The width is 44" for the door including left and right door frames.
The distance from the top of the door to the ceiling is 11".

The Entablature

1. For the entablature above the columns cut two pieces of poster board 11" x 22". Tape them together in back so your piece measures 22" x 44". Measure halfway up (5 1/2") on each side. Draw a line from each halfway point to the top center. Cut along lines.

2. Divide the entablature into a triangular pediment and a horizontal two-part section of sculpted frieze and plain architrave. Outline the triangle with 1" lines. You will have 1" lines up the roof slants (cornices) and 1" into the horizontal part. Divide the remaining 4" section in half.

3. From white corrugated paper cut eleven squares approximately 1 1/2" x 1 1/2". These are triglyphs. Cut eleven pieces 1 1/2" x 1/2". Arrange the triglyphs equally along the upper frieze part of the base. Glue in place. Arrange the small pieces under the dividing line and under the triglyphs in the architrave. Glue in place. We added more details and depth to our entablature by cutting and gluing on additional strips of cardboard. We also cut and glued several layers of cardboard sculpture to our pediment. Paint the entablature white to resemble marble. Set aside and let dry.
(continued on page 76)

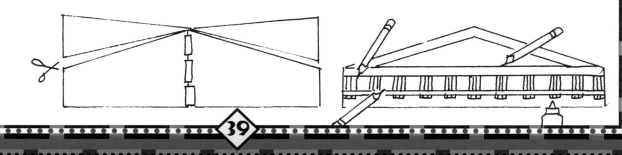

WAR SHIELDS

WAR SHIELDS

Materials: Railroad board 22" x 18", ruler, pencil, scissors, newspaper for pattern, brush, paints of choice.

1. Look at the different sizes and shapes of shields. There are many images to choose from, but the shapes are usually one of these three. Choose a shape and draw it on a folded piece of newspaper using a ruler and pencil to ensure its symmetry.
2. Trace the shape onto a piece of railroad board and cut it out. Paint the shield a color.
3. Here are a few common images from ancient shields:

4. Again, trace the shield shape onto a newspaper. With a marker draw the design onto the newspaper/shield. Cut out the design and trace around it on your cardboard shield. If a symmetrical design is chosen (such as a ***gorgon*** or crab—see ***gorgon*** pattern on page 71), fold the shield pattern in half. Draw half the design on the fold, and when it is cut there will be two matching sides. Trace around the design on the cardboard shield adding details such as legs, teeth, etc. A contemporary image might be chosen such as a cartoon character.
5. Paint the form on the shield. Cut a slit at the top and bottom of the shield, overlap the edges and staple to curve the shield. Add a cardboard, leather or rope strap to the back.

Ancient Greek city-states trained free-born men to defend their state whenever needed. Greeks who could afford horses joined the cavalry. Most served as foot soldiers called ***hoplites***. Body shields were carried by the ***hoplites***. The shields were made of bronze or leather to protect them from neck to thigh. The shield symbol represented the family or city. ***Hoplites*** had to buy their expensive armor and weapons, so most came from well-to-do families. The scary gorgon image was sculpted from stone, painted on surfaces and used often in the theater. The most famous gorgon was Medusa who had snakes for hair, huge teeth, and eyes that could turn people into stone. Greek mythology records that Perseus killed Medusa and chopped off her head. He then gave it to Athena to stick in the middle of her shield. Thus, the gorgon was popular on shields.

THE ETRUSCANS AND THE ROMANS

In 900 B.C. the earliest people in this region were the Villanovans, near Bologna in the northwest part of Italy. Their graves contained items of clay, bronze, iron, bone and amber.

By 700 B.C. the Etruscans (Tuscany) lived in the land called Etruria. Their exported mineral wealth of iron ore, copper, tin, lead and silver gave them exposure to the art and cultures of Greece, Phoenicia and Assyria.

Vestiges of this cosmopolitan people with a written language are most evident in their funeral rooms *(tumuli)*. Excavations reveal brilliantly painted walls of a handsome aristocracy enjoying feasting, dancing, hunting and games...all in outdoor settings rich in natural beauty.

The Etruscan loose city-states were unified under a king *(lucumon)* and seemed to be peaceful. Women fully participated in events, arm in arm with their husbands. When the Romans fought the Etruscans and assimilated them, their remarkable art was absorbed as well. The famous Capitoline Wolf was Etruscan. The suckling boys Romulus and Remus were not added until the Renaissance.

Rome

In 753 B.C. Rome was a small sleepy village on the Tiber River amidst its seven hills. The legend of its founding begins with Aeneas, a Trojan hero who escaped to Italy and founded a kingdom called Latium, the people being called Latins. King Numitor, a wicked descendant of Aeneas, had twin grandsons, Romulus and Remus. King Numitor was deposed by his brother who threw the babies into the Tiber river. The cradle was washed ashore and the twins were raised by a she-wolf until they were found by a shepherd who raised them. As adults they decided to build a city at the place they had been rescued. The brothers quarreled; Romulus killed Remus and was named Rome's first king in 753 B.C.

By 509 B.C. Rome went from a kingdom to a republic. Over the next 500 years the Romans conquered and absorbed the Etruscans and recognized the greatness of Greek culture and also absorbed it. In 260 B.C. the Punic Wars with the Phoenicians were waged.

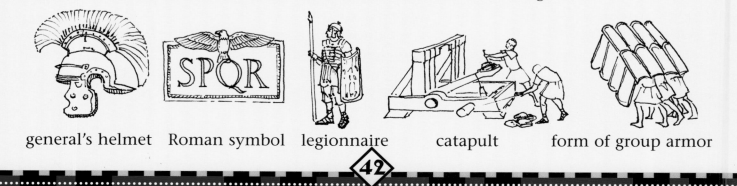

general's helmet   Roman symbol   legionnaire   catapult   form of group armor

The great Carthaginian general, Hannibal, crossed the alps with 36 elephants. By 146 B.C. Carthage was destroyed and Rome was the dominant power with great armies and battle strategies. The generals (e.g., Caesar) were more powerful than civic leaders. For 150 years peace reigned until Augustus defeated Mark Antony in 31 B.C. at the battle of Actium. By 27 B.C. the Senate had granted great powers to Augustus who then ruled the Roman Empire.

ROMAN CONTRIBUTIONS

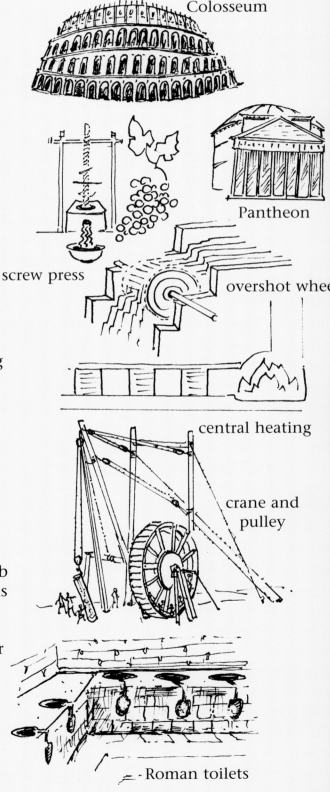

Colosseum

Pantheon

screw press

overshot wheel

central heating

crane and pulley

Roman toilets

At the peak of the Roman Empire a massive building program improved Rome with bridges and aqueducts that provided water for fountains, homes and bathhouses. Imperial architects built enormous public baths, Trajan's impressive Forum, the Colosseum, the Circus Maximus for chariot-racing which seated 250,000 people, and the domed Pantheon.

Most important inventions were borrowed from other civilizations. These were improved and adapted by brilliant Roman engineering. Slaves provided the labor.

Agriculture: The **screw press** was used for grapes and olives. The **undershot wheel** provided water power to mill grain, but the **overshot wheel** did not depend on the depth of the water and provided eight times the energy.

Concrete was invented in the second century B.C. using volcanic dust called *pozzolana*. It was faced with bricks when used for buildings.

Central heating was provided by *hypocausts*. The floor was supported on stacks of clay tiles. Hot air was forced from the furnace to heat up the floor. Only important rooms were heated.

Locks and keys were improved to secure doors.

Roads and bridges were surveyed with a *groma* (a plumb line) and a *dioptra* (a machine for surveying). Cofferdams were underwater bridge foundations of cement. Now, 2000 years later, many of these bridges are in use.
Cranes and pulleys were used for building as well as for unloading ships.

Pipes, baths, drains and sewers *allowed more water per person to flow into ancient Rome than into present-day New York City!!* Excess water from the baths flushed the public toilets, which had a row of seats over a channel of running water.

Other important inventions were in areas of metalworking, mining, medicine and shipbuilding.

ETRUSCAN TOMB PAINTING

AN ETRUSCAN TOMB PAINTING
A Group Project for at least 12 people

Materials: Enlargements of the Etruscan figures on page 79. Two sets of seven pieces of white school paper 10' x 4' (total 14 pieces), thin, middle and big brushes, sponge brushes, thinned tempera paint of all colors, pencils, containers for paints, newspaper, scissors, tape and stencils for the wave motif and ivy top border on page 78.

Twelve sixth graders produced the tomb painting working one to two hours, three times a week for a month. See their photo on the title page.

The background panels

1. Measure each panel 6" at the top for ivy border, 84" for main part, 6" for color band with wave, 6" for color band and bottom color band of plants. Decide on colors. Mix a big batch of each (especially the main part) and paint with fat sponge brushes or fat paint brushes. Study the Etruscan motifs on page 69. These panels should have birds, trees and bushes.

2. Students should work in pairs. They should choose the figure they wish to make from page 79. Have a thinnish person with unbaggy clothes lie on the white paper panel.
Have the artist pair adjust the feet, head and hands to replicate the Etruscan.
Carefully trace around the body. Draw in the features and details in pencil.
Remember to have the figures facing different directions.

3. After the figures have been painted with colorful clothing, jewelry, sandals, fancy hair, shawls, togas and capes, cut them out and mount with tape rolls on the outdoor panels that are already in place.

AN ETRUSCAN COLLECTION

AN ETRUSCAN COLLECTION
A Group Project for 4-5 people

Materials: A shallow lid at least 20" x 18" or a piece of matte board of the same size and colored on both sides, white school paper 18" x 12", markers of appropriate colors, colored pencils, tempera or acrylic paint, brushes, pencil, ruler, scissors, glue, salt dough recipe with ingredients of 2 cups flour, 1 cup salt, and 1 cup warm water.

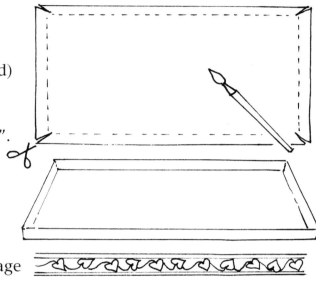

Making the container
Paint the lid a plain background color of brown, black, etc. If you use a piece of matte board (as we did) cut it to size on a paper cutter. Notch each corner diagonally an inch and score an inch or more from cut to cut so the edges can be bent and create a "box". Tape the corner with a tape you can paint or that blends with the color.

Making the Etruscan objects
Look at Etruscan patterns on page 69. Look at Etruscan art in available art books. Color copy an image that would work well in the shadow box.

Creating the river god head or the ram's head container
1. Make a batch of salt dough that can air dry or dry in a slightly warm oven. The markings on the container were made with wire in 600 B.C. They can be made with a fine-tipped marker after painting the salt dough form of the vessel.
2. Design the shadow box by moving items around. When you have a pleasing collage glue the bottom pattern pieces in place with paper cutouts as the next layer. Finally glue the relief objects and any pressed plants, etc. (Continued on page 77)

C

B

A

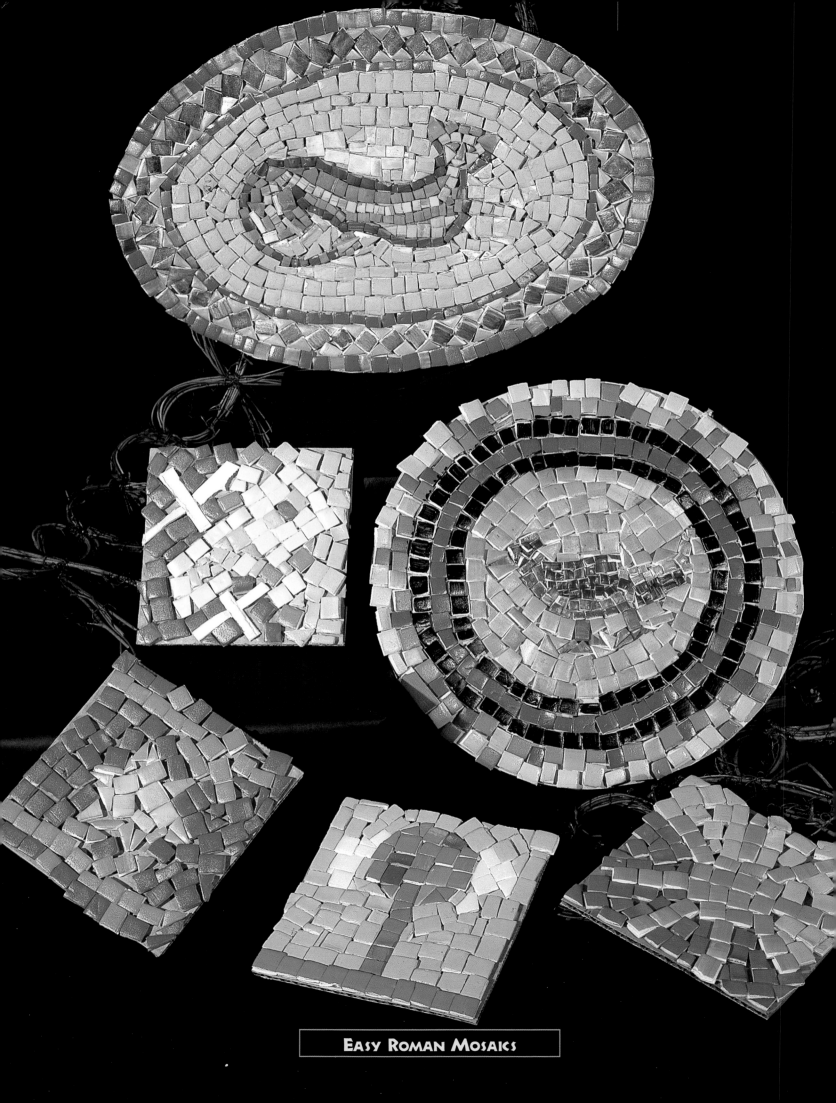

EASY ROMAN MOSAICS

EASY ROMAN MOSAICS

Materials: Styrofoam food trays in any color, cut cardboard shapes, glue, acrylic paint (traditional colors were olive green, brown, bright green, deep red, ocher, light blue, gray blue, white), brushes, scissors, planning paper.

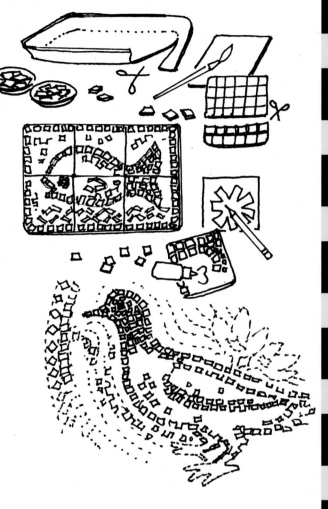

1. Preparation:
   a. Trim the curved edges from each tray.
   b. Paint Styrofoam with traditional colors or choose your own palette
   c. Cut dried, painted Styrofoam squares into 3/8" strips which are then cut into squares
   d. Put each color in an open container for easy access.

2. Look at mosaic patterns and designs below. Look at Roman mosaics in books. Design the mosaic on paper, remembering that borders are important.

To the adult: Individuals could do a mosaic or a group could do a larger one by gridding a projected mosaic and dividing it into sections. These sections could be done and then assembled into a whole.

3. Draw mosaic ideas on a planning paper, keeping the central image <u>simple</u> with a contrasting background.

4. Use a 5" cardboard square, a paper-plate-size surface or any shape including oval, hexagon, or round for the surface. Cover a small section with glue and put your Styrofoam painted squares in place. Snip halves or parts for irregular spaces.

When we think of Roman mosaics we usually recall floor mosaics that have been preserved because of the durable material. The first mosaic floors were made of natural pebbles, dating from the 8th to 7th centuries B.C. Greeks used light and dark pebbles to show off the figures. Strips of lead or terra-cotta clay outlined important parts of the design. Pebbles and stone chips were eventually combined. Stones as small as 1/4" were commonly used in mosaics in Pompeii and Herculaneum. Marble chips were found in stonemasons' rubble piles. Throughout the Roman empire stunning floor mosaics were made from local stone or imported materials. England has many fine examples of mosaic floors using local stone.

A ROMAN BANNER

A ROMAN BANNER
A Group Project for 9-10 people

Materials: Two pieces of white school paper 8' x 8', samples of Roman patterns and motifs on pages 68 and 70, markers of dominant colors, ruler, pencils, carbon paper, black tea bags or strong coffee, sponges, scissors, a 3' long piece of 1" dowel, 5' of string to use with the dowel.

1. Prepare one of the sheets of paper by measuring nine 8" squares and long paper borders 2 1/2" wide. After the paper has been marked with a pencil and it is on the floor or a table, dab it with soaked black tea bags or sponges dipped in 1/2 cup of very strong coffee (coffee leaves a smell). This should give it an old, aged look.

2. When the paper has dried, cut out the nine squares and the border strips. Enlarge the patterns and motifs on page 68. The borders range from 1" to 2" wide. Borders can be transmitted to the square by using a strip of carbon paper and tracing over the design or rubbing pencil on the border back and tracing the design with the graphite of the pencil lead acting as a "carbon".

3. This system works if the motifs and borders are to be duplicated. Artists can also create their own adapted borders and motifs from the study of Roman art.

4. Print the borders with ruled color markers and print the design in the middle with Jiffy foam or a potato print. We used both.

5. Assemble the squares on the second piece of 8' paper. Glue in place with the printed borders framing the squares. Fold the top over for a banner support and glue or tape in place. Insert a wooden dowel with string to hold the banner.

The borders and motifs for this banner were taken from authentic samples of Roman wall paintings and mosaics. This same banner activity could depict an Ancient Greek theme or Mycenaean or Cretan design. These cultures are rich in visual ideas for a group project.

A Portrait Mask

A PORTRAIT MASK

Materials: A roll of plaster of paris bandage used for casts by the medical profession, a bowl of water, scissors, towels, plastic wrap, acrylic paints optional.

Preparing the model

1. Cut bandage strips in half making strips about 1" wide. Cut a few strips 4" to 6" long but mostly use 2" to 3" pieces.

2. Have model lie on floor or table and place towel under the head. Cover face crossways with two sections of plastic wrap each about 10" long. Cover upper and lower sections of the face overlapping in middle and **leaving nostrils clear.** Keep plastic covering as smooth as possible.

Applying the plaster bandage

Models must close their eyes and lie as still as possible without talking for the several minutes of application and 5 minutes of set-up time.

3. Dip first strip into water to activate plaster. Lightly remove excess water and lay strip over face. Smooth out wrinkles. Cover forehead and sides of face with long strips. Use shorter ones for front of face and features. Gently smooth as you go. Keep nostril area dry and clear.

4. Carefully cover all of face. Try to apply no more than two layers so features remain clear.

5. Wait about 5 minutes for plaster of paris to set. Carefully lift mask and remove plastic wrap. Cover nostril holes with several pieces of wrap.

6. Lightly trim the uneven edges of the mask with scissors. Paint or leave white to resemble the marble portrait sculptures of Greece and Rome.

A Pompeiian Wall Painting

A POMPEIIAN WALL PAINTING

Materials: Two pieces of white school paper 36" wide and 48" long, pencils, yard-sticks, permanent black marker with big tip, brushes of all sizes, glue, water-based paint and containers, newspapers, scissors, Pompeiian red mixed paint, gold paint is optional.

Roman wall paintings found in Pompeii and Herculaneum often had patterned borders, faux "marble columns" on each side and favored a rich orange-red color now called Pompeiian-red (1/2 red, 1/2 orange with some brown). This rich color surrounded the central painting which was usually a landscape, a portrait, an event, a symbol or a deity. These many-sized paintings often lined important rooms in homes of the wealthy.

1. This is a good "team" project. Four or five parts of the final painting can be done as separate units and then glued together on the cut white paper backing. In the photographed sample five different students took:

    a. the central landscape and surrounding color
    b. the columns
    c. the top gold pattern

The two bottom borders were designed by two students. A supervisor approved the rough color sketch the student research had produced.

2. Once the design has been researched, a rough color sketch with measurements should be made and approved. Measure and cut the first piece of white paper into sections according to the plan. Each team member takes a section to produce. Remember to protect painting surfaces with newspaper. Thin the paint except for the

brilliant Pompeiian red. The original paintings have a washed look.

3. Glue the parts to the second piece of white paper providing glue-drying pressure with books and magazines.

Pompeii was a prosperous coastal city overlooking the Bay of Naples and its busy port. Mt. Vesuvius was six miles away. Pompeii was connected to Rome by the *Via Appian* (the Appian Way), a fine road built for defense purposes. On August 24, 79 A.D. tragedy struck when Mt. Vesuvius erupted and buried Pompeii and nearby Herculaneum under a blanket of ash. Then 1700 years later Pompeii was excavated and found to be almost perfectly preserved.

GREEK AND ROMAN COINS

GREEK AND ROMAN COINS

Materials: Heavy paper plates, plastic squeeze bottle or school glue bottle with narrow spout, plaster of paris, cement for mixing or spackling compound, gold brush paint or spray paint, small brush and black, orange or brown paint.

1. Mix the compound (according to directions) that is going to set up in the paper plate. Allow it time to dry overnight. The surface should be hard and white or gray if cement was used.

2. Research coins and find an image. It can be greatly enlarged on a copy machine to fit the paper plate or can be drawn from the original.

3. If an enlargement is to be used, draw the important features with a sharp point, incising the paper plate surface. Or, use a pencil to draw the image onto the surface.

4. Make a flour mixture and pour into a plastic squeeze bottle or use a glue bottle with a good spout. The recipe for the liquid in the bottle is: 1/2 c. water, 1/2 c. flour, 2 ts. alum. Mix in a blender or a bowl using a good tool. **You do not want lumps.**

5. Squeeze the liquid onto the lines on the surface. Let the paste dry overnight. It should create a relief of the coin image. Spray it gold or paint it gold. Add color with your fingertip or a brush. Our images represent a shrimp, Alexander the Great, Athena's owl and one of the Caesars. They are adapted from museum pieces.

Ancient Greeks and Romans had beautiful coins. Most often they were decorated with the profiles of the current ruler just as our penny has Abraham Lincoln. Coins were probably invented at the end of the 6th century B.C. in Asia Minor. The idea spread to the Greek colonies in Ionia and mainland Greece. Only Spartans resisted adopting the coin. They used iron rods for trade for another 300 years. The earliest coins were lumps of a mixture of gold and silver. Eventually coins were mostly silver and were made in a standard flat, round shape.

LOVE

ROMAN LETTER

HAPPINESS IS THE ABILITY TO PRACTICE APPRECIATION OR LOVE

WALKED TEN MILES TWO PAIR SOCKS

AD 122 HADRIAN WALL

THE WRITTEN TRADITION

THE WRITTEN TRADITION

***Materials: (A) 22" x 28" white poster board (makes sixteen 5 1/2" x 7" tablets),
black wet tea bags, toothpicks with points cut off, scissors, black tempera paint.
(B) Styrofoam meat tray in white or yellow, brown twine, pencil, paper punch.
(C) Styrofoam meat tray, Popsicle sticks, pencil, planning paper the same size as
styro tablet. (D) Manila folder aged with paint or tea, scissors.***

(A) Make "faux papyrus" by dyeing poster board
with tea. Cover tablet with horizontal strokes.
Let dry. Make spaced vertical strokes. Let dry.
Refer to page 81 for written alphabet. Plan what
to write. Dip end of toothpick stylus into tempera
paint and write a message.

(B) Make a "wax" tablet book using two or more
meat market Styrofoam trays. Trim the edges.
Punch two holes in same place on each table
Refer to page 81 for alphabet. Plan the message.
Using a pencil as a "stylus," incise words into
the "wax". Assemble pages in order, punch holes
and tie with twine.

(C) Formal Roman capitals (majuscules)
used for important declarations were actually
"carved in stone". The 2" high majuscules,
however, will be carved in foam. A styrofoam tray
and two Popsicle sticks are needed. The two sticks
have three different uses: Tool A is needed for its curved
end only. The second has two purposes: Tool B
has a flat end, the curved end having been cut off,
and a 2" straight edge. Use tool C for horizontal,
vertical and diagonal parts of the majuscules.
Curved parts are drawn with a corner of Tool B/C.
On a planning paper write a word or brief
message with 2" letters. It must fit the styrofoam
tray. Find the Roman majuscules on page 81
and "carve" the message by pressing hard into
the foam with the tools. Finish by incising a decorative border.

(D) Make a Roman soldier's accordion tablet by cutting the aged manila folder into rectangles
3" x 5". Using the toothpick and paint write a daily journal. Punch holes on each end and
connect with twine. Many of these personal records were found when Hadrian's wall was
excavated.

(continued on page 81)

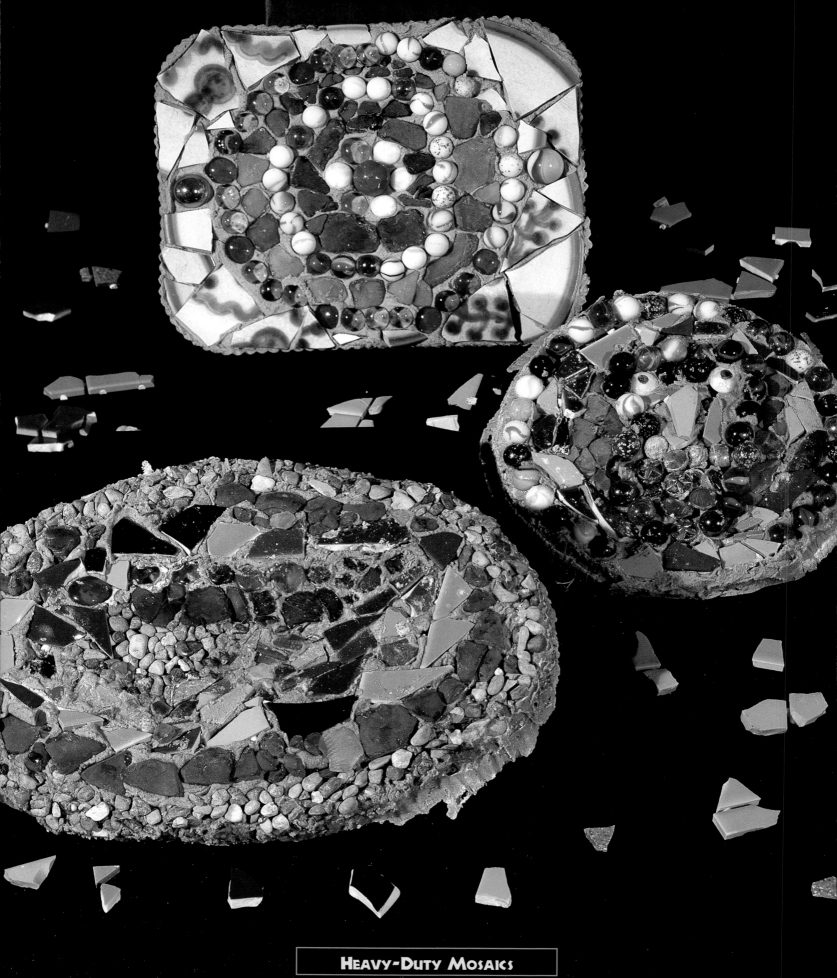

HEAVY-DUTY MOSAICS

HEAVY-DUTY MOSAICS

Materials: Powdered cement or plaster of paris for mixing, water, a bowl, aluminum pans in desired size: pie tin, lasagna pan, pizza pan, etc., broken dishes, tile, mosaic stones from craft store, sea glass, marbles, plant pebbles, buttons, shells, etc. will all create interesting mosaics.

Depending on the smoothness and safety of the surfaces of this mosaic, it can go on a horizontal surface (garden, tabletop, floor spot) or, if its pieces have sharp edges, it can hang on or lean against a wall.

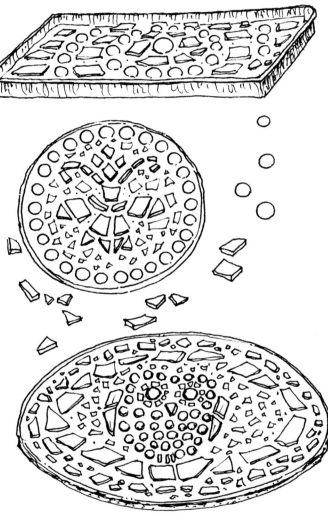

1. Mix the cement or plaster and immediately pour it into the prepared aluminum container. If it is plaster you must work **very fast** as it will set up in 10-15 minutes. If you mix it with a little more water it will set up more slowly but not be as strong.

2. It takes the cement several hours to set up so there is not a sense of rush. Start with the center, which might be an especially showy ceramic piece, and work out to the edges.

3. General design or a figure? We attempted an owl on one mosaic and a fish on a second and a general rectangular design in the third. Clearly the design worked best. These spaces are too small to create a recognizable form.

4. After your cement and mosaic pieces have firmly set up, you can unmold the piece from the aluminum.

The technique of using small pieces of stone, glass, pottery shards, shells and a variety of brightly colored materials was used in wall encrustations. The technique was as old as 300 B.C. when wall mosaics were found in Mesopotamia. Floor mosaics were common, but it has now been determined that wall and vault mosaics were also in Pompeii and Nero's palace. They were made of cut glass. Early mosaics were fountain supports or decorated natural grottos known as *nymphaeums.*

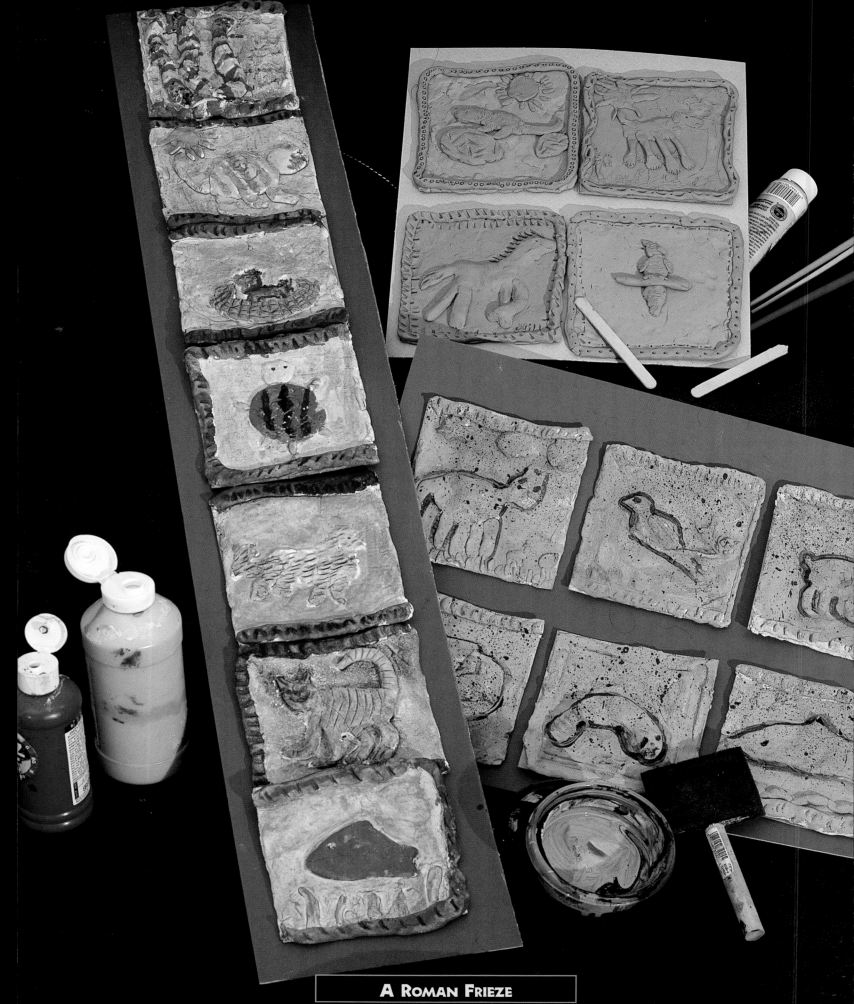

A ROMAN FRIEZE

A ROMAN FRIEZE

Materials: Terra-cotta plasticene (molding clay) and cardboard. Salt dough clay recipe, tools for texture and patterns such as a nail, wooden craft stick, scissor point. For painted dough tiles use any water-based paint, tiny and medium bristled brushes, water, waxed paper.

Three variations on individual tiles were produced by second graders with pets as the theme (see pattern page 82). Note: Our photograph had to be vertical but *finished tiles should be mounted side by side in a horizontal line as the Romans wrapped them around their handsome buildings and rooms.* One set of tiles is clay and will never harden. The next two tile sets are salt dough which will air harden: one set is "marbleized" and the other painted. All have interesting border patterns. The salt dough recipe: 2 c. flour, 1 c. water, 1 c. salt. Mix and cook until a workable ball. Bake projects in 200 degree oven until hard (2-4 hours). Matte board and glue for mounting is optional.

1. Talk about the subject of the frieze: sports, friends, important events, plants, structures, etc. We chose animals.

2. Choose your subject and plan how it is to be presented. Cut 5" square cardboard and draw the tile subject on it. Spread the baseball-size molding material on waxed paper. Roll with a rolling pin or your hand to 1/4". Make it 5" square. Save some clay for the border.

3. Make the tile by studying the drawing. "Draw" the design on the clay with a sharp point. Carefully lift up the square and place it on the cardboard square. Make the texture, built-up parts, etc. more interesting with the sharp-pointed tools.

4. When you are satisfied with the design, make "clay worms" and place them around the tile as a border. Make a design on the border. Let the salt dough dry overnight.

5. "Marble" it by painting it a light gray and then spatter paint black with a fat dry brush. Stand back 12"-15" to make tiny specks, or paint the tile with bright colors.

6. Glue tiles in a horizontal line to a heavy cardboard such as matte board and put a pliable book on them as a glue-press overnight.

The Roman frieze was a presentation of information. It was an important service, glorified deeds and leaders, recorded family and national history and recounted religious rituals. These stone relief sculptures could get clear messages to the people in a direct visual form of a patriotic message.

Two Greek Theatrical Masks

Materials: A Chinette™ oval plate for each mask, a full paint palette, brushes, paper strips, flour and water for papier-mache', black or brown raffia, scissors, glue, a paint stick handle for each mask, pencil, masking tape, hot glue gun.

Greek theaters were open-air amphitheaters with seating for as many as 10,000 to 20,000 spectators. Because actors (always men) were far away, they wore enlarged masks with exaggerated features and funnel-type lips that acted as megaphones. The masks were made of fabric stiffened with plaster, an almost exact process as this activity. The actors wore a mask that represented a mood or characteristic (sad, silly, happy, etc.). Brightly colored clothes also gave clues as to the figures. Dull, subdued clothes were worn for the tragic roles. Acrobat, bird and animal costumes were sometimes worn by chorus members. A stick is one mask support, but actors needed their hands so a variety of head attachments were used.

Woman's mask

1. The cardboard paper plate is positioned horizontally. Pencil large holes for eyes, a big, gaping mouth and the nose. Cut out the eye holes. Cut a slit for the mouth, notch the upper and lower lips and fold them up to help form the funnel-shaped mouth. Cut the nose triangle and fold; check for size and position on the face and use masking tape to hold it in place.

2. Prepare the flour and water (see page 29 for flour and water ratio) for papier-mache' work. Tear or cut several 1-1/2" paper strips from recycled paper, paper towels or newspaper. Think about cheeks (balls of paper), eyebrows, protruding chin, ears, built-up forehead, etc. Create these with paper balls or long rolls of paper taped in place and then apply papier-mache over the form to create a strong, smooth surface. Let the piece dry overnight.

3. Paint the face with light flesh colors but paint bright lips and cheeks and dark eyebrows so the audience can see the features.

4. Add long strips of raffia from a front hair part with a hot glue gun or white glue with weights until it has dried. After the "hair" has been attached add earrings, a crown or wreath, ribbon, etc. Hot glue the paint stick to the mask back.

(continued on page 72)

ARCHIMEDES WATER SCREW

Materials: A piece of 5 1/2" square poster board, 3/4" x 8" garden hose, 1/2" x 12" heavy rope, masking tape, scissors, a quart milk carton, half-pint milk carton, 1 cup uncooked rice.

1. Curve poster board square by rolling loosely around hose. Do not fold.

2. Make a gob of tape and attach to one end of rope. On one opening of the hose, secure this sticky end 2–2 1/2" of cord.

3. Wrap rope around hose so wrap is spaced like a screw. Tape rope end to hose about 2" from hose end.

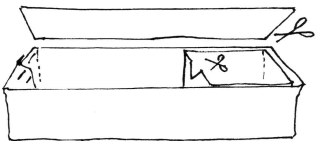

4. Cut a short piece of tape. Comfortably wrap cardboard around screw assembly and secure with tape. Add more tape along full length of tube. Trim a curved section to form a scoop at the back end.

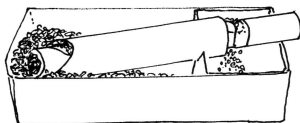

5. Cut top panel from quart carton. Flatten pointed top and staple. Cut top from small carton so it is 2" high. Cut a notch to one side of it. The notch will support the tube in its diagonal position.

6. Set small box into large one with notch toward center. Pour rice into far end of large carton. Turn your screw assembly to see which way to raise the rice. Insert into tube and set into rice. Hold tube stationary and turn your Archimedes screw to "move" water from place to place.

The Greek scientist Archimedes designed the water screw in the 3rd century B.C. This simple machine could raise water from lower to higher levels. It could empty the flooded hold of a large ship or move water for farming purposes.

THE ROMAN ARCH

Materials: 2" x 2" x 12" foam (we used green), poster board, about 10 toothpicks, table knife, scissors, masking tape, black Sharpie marker, pattern on page 83.

1. Tape square pattern to foam and score both sides by tracing over lines with table knife. Divide into four supporting pier blocks each 2" x 2".

2. Next score both sides of *arch, lintel* and *abutment* using pattern parts. Cut the lintel first using a ruler to guide your knife. Alternately working from front to back carefully cut foam. With marker, note sequence number on each edge of arch section or *voussoir*.

3. Cut the two abacus slabs. These are wider than the four pier blocks and will hold up the curved scaffolding which supports our arch during construction.

4. On the poster board cut out the frame of base box from pattern. Tape corners. Our base box supports the pier blocks.

5. Cut out scaffolding from pattern. Fold on dotted lines and tape tab in place.

6. Set support piers at either end of base box. Secure with toothpicks. Add abacus on each and secure with toothpicks.
Stone construction provides pressure from weight (thrust) which holds pier blocks together. Our lightweight foam does not have such a thrust.

7. Set scaffolding on edge of each abacus between piers. Begin adding the voussoirs from side to side and placing, last of all, the keystone! Remove scaffolding.

8. On either side of arch, position abutment pieces and toothpick in place. Abutments receive pressure or thrust from a curved arch and keep the arch from slipping sideways.

9. Finally, place and secure the arch top.

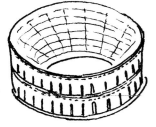

An arch is a curved architectural form that spans an opening. Romans used arches for many purposes: triumphal arches, theaters and amphitheaters with arched entryways that supported tiered seating for thousands, and arched bridges that extended roads over rivers and valleys and supported aqueducts.

A ROMAN AQUEDUCT

Materials: An egg carton, poster board, masking tape, paper towel cylinder, glue, scissors, ruler, pencil, Kix cereal.

1. Mark a diagonal line with a ruler and four attached egg carton sections from the highest part of the cup to the lowest. Keep the three arches between each cup. Cut away the excess. Cut out pattern for cover of carton cups. Slightly curve middle of cover to accommodate the curved cylinder. Fold and glue tabs to sides of cups.

2. Shorten cylinder to 9". Cut opening in towel cylinder. Tape pattern circle over back of cylinder. Attach cylinder to carton cover.

3. Pour cereal into opening and watch results of gravity flow from your inclined aqueduct.

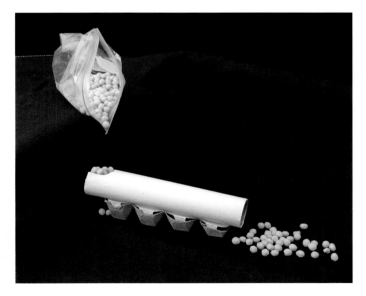

The Romans constructed aqueducts to carry water from natural streams to Rome. These were inclined surfaces, tunnels and pipes to keep water flowing downhill to reservoirs and from those to private homes, public baths and fountains. One of the finest examples of a Roman aqueduct construction is the Pont du Gard in Nimes, France. It took 35 years to build and was finished in 14 A.D.

TROJAN PATTERNS

MYCENAEAN PATTERNS

GREEK/ROMAN PATTERNS

CULTURAL PATTERNS

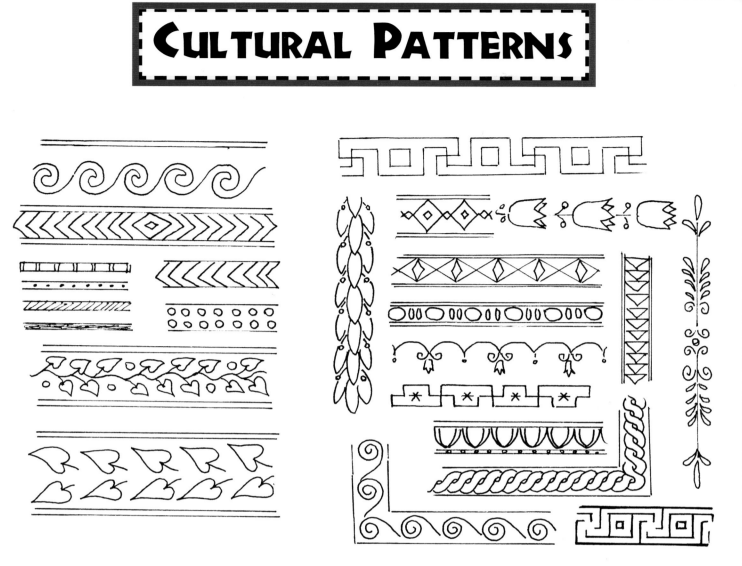

ETRUSCAN PATTERNS

GREEK/ROMAN PATTERNS

MYCENAEAN PATTERNS

IMAGES FOR
ROMAN
BANNER

GORGON SHIELD
PATTERN

TROJAN HORSE PATTERN

Some parts are cut double.

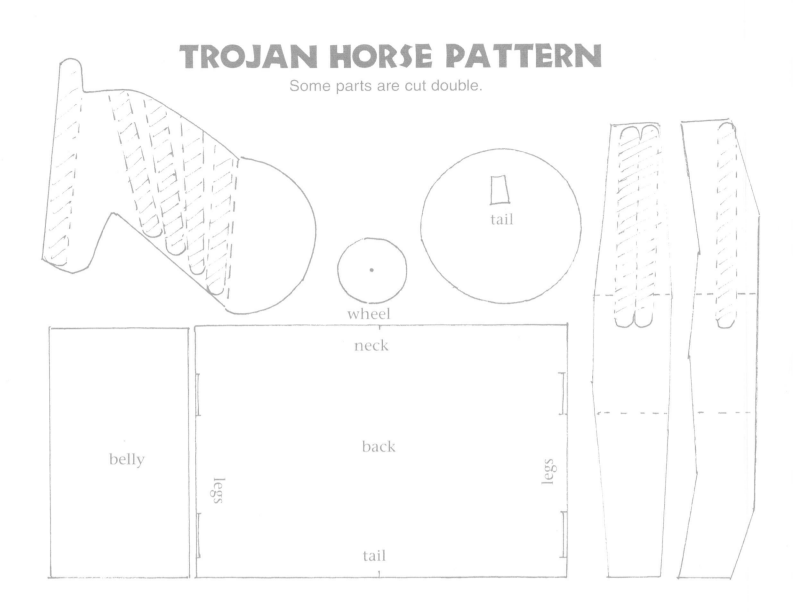

(Two Greek Theatrical Masks - continued from page 64)

Bearded man mask

1. Follow the directions as for the women's mask except position the mask vertically.
2. Paint the face much more ruddy with orange and red in the flesh palette.
3. Add cut brown or black paper strips for the hair and beard or papier-mache' strips you will paint.

The Western concept of drama is deeply rooted in Ancient Greece. The theater was one of the few public places open to women. Plays called "tragedies" told stories of heroes and dealt with serious moral subjects. "Comedies" presented important citizens in amusing, unlikely situations and made fun of the gods. Specific masks often had the features of recognizable people in the town or city-state.

(The Parthenon - continued from page 27)

4. The inner cella box is optional but adds to the authenticity of the Parthenon. The cella will have a porch at each end with six columns. The inner box is 17" x 7" x 7". Remove short flaps and measure and mark where columns will stand. The porch columns will be the same height as the colonnade columns. Cut spaces between columns. Mark side spaces behind porch columns. Cut and fold back so there is an aisle behind the 6 columns. This is the porch. Take the two 6" x 6" partitions and cut a center door opening in each. Glue the partitions in place on the front of the folded flaps at each porch end. Take the 6" x 9" partition. Score and fold back a 1" flap on each side. Glue in place to make a large room and a small one. The large east-facing room was the sanctuary of the grand statue of Athena.

5. Steps to the Parthenon are graduated strips of cardboard stacked together and glued. Styrofoam steps would also work. When your stairs are high enough, measure and cut the lengths so they surround the Parthenon. Cut corners at a 45 degree angle. Fit steps in place and tape underneath to one another and to buildings. With white paint cover the colonnade, cella and steps. The Parthenon roof was made of marble tiles. Let the paint dry.

6. Dramatic sculpture honoring the goddess Athena decorated the entablature of the Parthenon colonnade and cella. Look at the Doric Doorway activity and make decorations by cutting paper to size for the triangular ends and two side entablatures of the colonnade. Our side strips are 1" x 21". Cut frieze strips for the cella. Decorate and paint and glue colonnade to colonnade and cella. Close cella flaps with tape and place inside colonnade. Choose roof of colonnade.

The architects of Classical Greece built according to strict mathematical rules to give their public buildings a feeling of balance, simplicity and elegance. The Greek city-states commissioned architects and sculptors to construct magnificent public buildings and monuments. Most of them were made of marble or limestone with wooden beams to support the roof which was covered with tiles made of marble or a clay called terra-cotta. Temples such as the Parthenon were the focus for religious feeling and local pride. The Greeks built the Parthenon without the help of cranes or cement.

(Centaur, Stag and Bull - continued from page 13)

The Bull (easiest of the animals):
The only tubes in the bull are the 3" body tube and the 2" head tube. The front and back legs, tail and horns are cardboard taped to the body. The head is then taped to the cardboard. Make the head look like a bull, not a horse or a deer or a dog. Study the bull's head in pictures.

Horse and stag figures made of clay were found in early Athens, 1100 B.C. Then 200 years later, they were being drawn on vases. The bull, a sacred symbol of the Minoan religion, inspired the Mycenaean figure. They created clay forms from most natural objects such as birds and sealife. The patterns are typical of Mycenaean designs.

(Musical Instruments - contuied from page 35)

Kithara (similar to a lyre)

Materials: 2 pieces 20" x 20" of heavy cardboard. Gold paint or marker, 12 small nails, 20-30 ft. of monofilament, brown and black paint, brush, strong scissors, glue.

1. Draw the kithara shape on the fold of a newspaper. Cut it out. Trace the shape around the two pieces of heavy cardboard. Cut each out.

2. With a 1" x 12" cardboard piece as a crossbar, glue the two cardboards together and put weights on them while they dry. Be sure the crossbar at the top is straight.

3. Paint everything brown with touches of black.

4. Pencil the design. Go over the design with gold paint or marker (or yellow or white if gold is unavailable).

5. Glue a 1/2" painted cardboard piece at bottom middle. Hammer 5-6 nails in crossbar and 5-6 nails in cardboard square. Stretch the filament by twining it around the nails. Tie it off, keeping the tension tight.

Judging from vase paintings, the ancient Greeks enjoyed music at most events. The *kithara* was an elaborate stringed wooden instrument similar to a lyre. It is plucked with a pick like object. The *timpanon* was an early version of the tambourine. Two pipes at a time were played as well. The turtle-shell harp is portrayed often, played by men and women.

ATHENA'S
OWL
PATTERN

VASE
PATTERNS

(**Doric Doorway** - continued from page 39)

1. Cut a poster board back strip for each column. The complete length will be 80" high by 8" wide. When you have cut and taped these two long strips, taper 2" from one side of each. Start at the top so your final backing strips are 6" wide at the top and 8" wide at the bottom.

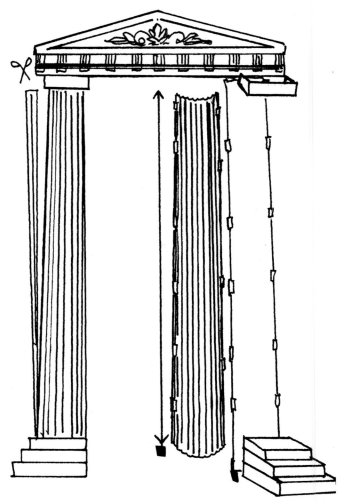

2. Stack your box lid stepped platform. Ours are three 7" x 9 1/2" lids (A-6 envelope size). Our bottom step is full-size. The middle step is cut to 8" x 5" and the top step is 3 1/2" of the short end of the lid. Using a total of six lids, make two stepped platforms and tape together. The platform sides near the doorway need to be even. Away from the doorway they are graduated.

3. Atop each of the columns is a capital. From a single box lid cut 2 1/2" off each end. You now have two capitals 2 1/2" x 7".

4. Position your poster board backing strips by attaching one to each door frame. Press a stepped platform against each backing strip on the floor and tape securely in place.

5. Now measure the distance between the top of your stepped platform and the top of your door opening. Subtract 1 1/2" for the capital. This is the height of your column shaft. Our shaft is 73 1/2" high by 11" wide. Now taper one side of each so each measures 9" at the top and 11" at the bottom. Set the corrugated shaft on the stepped platform and curve around the poster board backing. Tape column edges securely around the back of the poster board. Your columns will probably need two or three stacked sections to reach 73 1/2". The Greeks stacked stone sections for their columns.

6. Place box lid capital onto column top and tape in place. Center the entablature over the doorway and columns and attach to door frame and wall. Congratulations!! You have made a magnificent Greek Doric doorway.

(**Etruscans Collection** - continued from page 47)

Dancing boy from a Tarquinian tomb

Etruscan tombs are rooms under the ground. Many have been restored. When visiting them you walk down a crude set of dirt stairs to a viewing window. Above the ground there is a mound or earth box indicating that a tomb exists. These rooms are lined with painted walls of colorful, seemingly happy scenes of Etruscans at play in the out-of-doors. The handsome, tunic draped people are feasting, singing, dancing, playing games, hunting and visiting. This handsome young boy is dancing with a female partner.

Painted borders

    A.   This is a popular border found on vase amphoras and bordering some tombs. It is from the 7th century B.C.

    B.   This animal pattern is from the included vase image. It has an interesting resemblance to Anasazi and Fremont prehistory people in the American Southwest.

    C.   The pattern of hearts on a vine is on most pottery. It was inspired by ivy.

    D.   This chevron pattern is found as a clothing border in a tomb and on an amphora.

The ram's head, heavily incised container

The symmetry of this three-dimensional vessel is appealing. Both ends have a similar neck: one end is a ram's head and at the opposite end is a pouring spout. The carefully scratched designs on the surface were popular with Etruscans. If a surface was hard and dark it was often incised.

Achelos, the River God plaque

This terra-cotta plaque was placed at the head end of a burial sarcophagus to ward off evil.

The handsome couple

Probably the most famous example of Etruscan art, this married couple is carved on the lid of their tomb. She is wearing a hat that conveys status. Their smiles and intimate posture give a sense of happiness. His fit masculinity is typical of the Etruscans.

The pretty young girl

Women were important in Etruscan life. The Greeks and Romans were astonished at the status of women who sat next to their husbands in public and private places such as theaters and games. The wives of Etruscan kings often paved the way for their husbands to gain their thrones and exerted great political influence. This terra-cotta piece is among many that show Etruscan girls and women as favorite subjects for artists.

ETRUSCAN TOMB PATTERNS

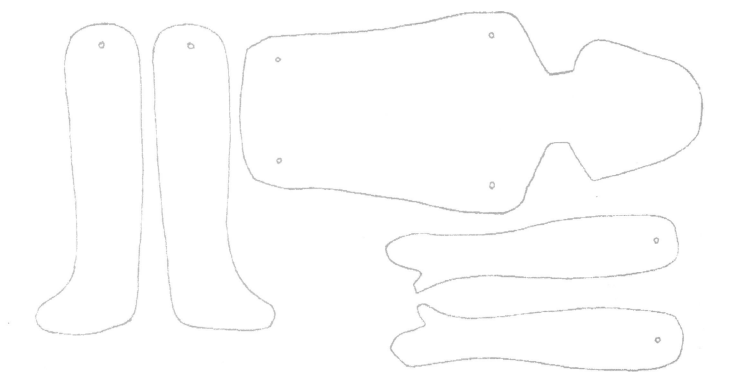

THREE TOY PATTERNS

(**Three Toys** - continued from page 29)
Playing with a whip and top goes back thousands of years. Greek children and adult women played with tops. Dolls and the clay pig rattle were found in tombs. The future of a baby rested in the hands of its father. If the baby was a weak girl or if the family could not afford to keep it, the father might abandon it by leaving it in the open air to die.

If a baby was finally accepted by its family and named on the tenth day, the upbringing was good. Evidence of many toys has been found in children's graves. Boys attended school and girls were taught domestic skills at home. At the age of 12 or 13 children dedicated their toys to the god Apollo and the goddess Artemis, signifying their entering into adulthood.

A B C D E F G H I J K L M N O P Q R S T U V W X Y Z

A B C D E F G H I J K L M N O P Q R S T U V W X Y Z

(The Written Tradition - continued from page 59)

Our alphabet came from the Roman alphabet which was based on the Greek one which evolved from the Phoenicians. Romans wrote on leather, pottery and wooden tablets covered with wax. They used a stylus for incising letters which was pointed on one end and blunt on the other end for erasing. They also wrote on papyrus with a brush or a reed pen which needed constant sharpening. Ink was made from lamp black, water and a gum binder. The first paged books from about 300 B.C. were sets of wax tablets connected by a cord.

Carved letters were more formal than the rapidly written personal and business ones. The magnificent Roman capitals carved in stone on Trajan's 100 foot high column in Rome at the end of the first century A.D. are still the prototype for monument inscriptions.

Our letter forms are based on Roman manuscript letters of 100 A.D. The letters J, K, U, and W were not used then. Although Roman writing did not separately space letters into words, dots effectively separate the letters and words.

ANIMAL
IMAGES

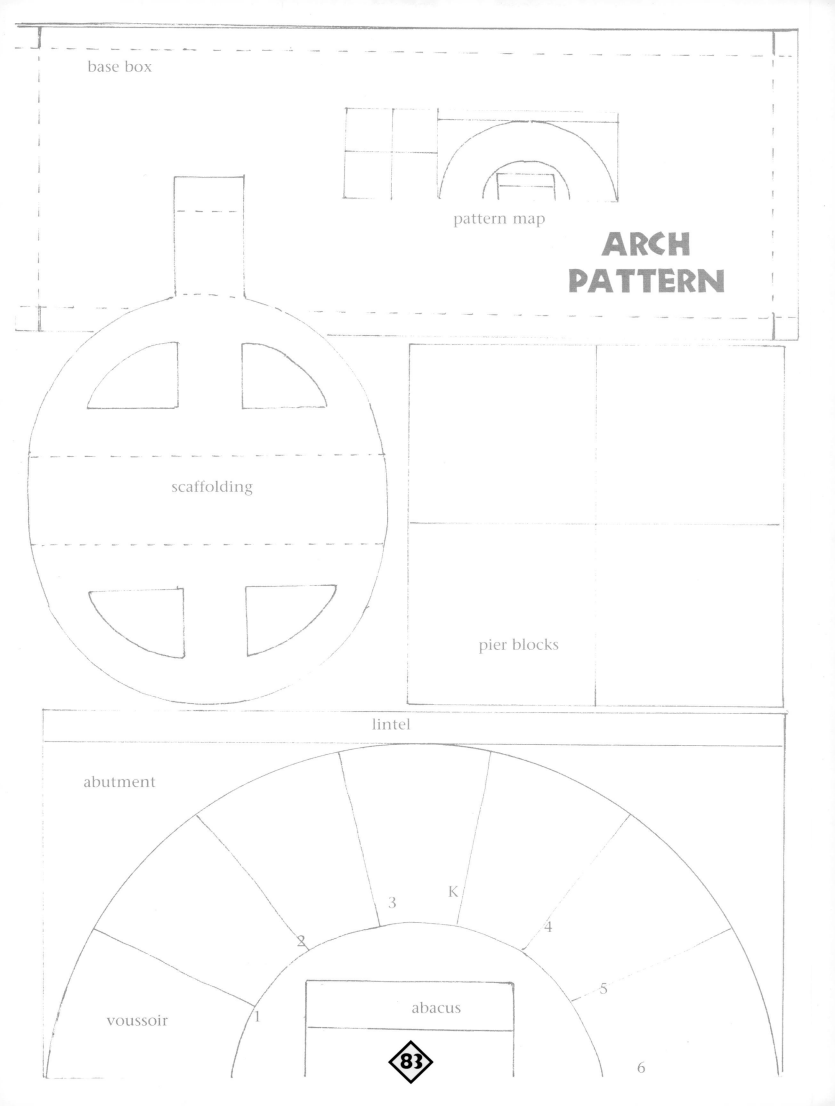

base box

pattern map

ARCH PATTERN

scaffolding

pier blocks

lintel

abutment

K

3

2

4

5

voussoir

1

abacus

6

MINOTAUR MASK PATTERN

WORDS ASSOCIATED WITH GREEK-ROMAN MYTHOLOGY

WORD	DEFINITION	NAMED FOR
Adonis	handsome young man	Adonis, youth beloved of Venus
aeolian harp	box with strings played by the wind	Aeolus, god of the winds
ambrosial	deliciously fragrant	ambrosia, the food of the gods
Apollo	handsome young man	Apollo, god of the sun
arachnid	spider	Arachne, who defied Minerva in a weaving contest
atlas	book of maps	Atlas, a Titan who carried the heavens on his shoulders
aurora borealis	northern lights	Aurora, goddess of the dawn
calliope	steam organ	Calliope, Muse of epic or heroic poetry
cereal	grain, especially breakfast food	Ceres, goddess of grain and harvest
chimerical	fantastic, unreal	Chimera, a fire-breathing monster
cupidity	strong desire	Cupid, god of love
echo	repeated sound	Echo, talkative wood nymph
halcyon	tranquil, happy	Alcyone, changed into a kingfisher
harpy	greedy or grasping person	Harpies, hideous winged monsters
helium	element first found on sun	Helios, ancient sun god
herculean	of great size and strength	Hercules, god of strength
hermetic	completely sealed	Hermes, often associated with magic
hyacinth	flower	Hyacinthus, beautiful youth
hygiene	science of health	Hygeia, goddess of health
hypnosis	sleep-like state	Hypnos, god of sleep
iridescent	having rainbow colors	Iris, goddess of the rainbow
January	month	Janus, two-headed god of doorways
jovial	hearty, genial cheerful	Jove (jupiter) king of the gods
Junoesque	stately and regal	Juno, queen of the gods
labyrinthine	complicated, puzzling	Labyrinth, the maze of Crete
March	month	Mars, god of war
May	month	Mail, goddess of incense and growth
mercurial	changeable, fickle	Mercury, god of speed, commerce
music	a pleasing sequence of sounds	Muses, goddesses of arts, science and literature
nectarine	fruit	nectar, the drink of the gods
ocean	body of salt water	Oceanus, a lonely Titan
Odyssey	an extended wandering	Odysseus, Greek warrior against Troy
panic	sudden, hysterical fear	Pan, woodland god who often frightened shepherds
Phaeton	four-wheeled carriage	Phaethon, who unsuccessfully drove the chariot of the sun
procrustean	securing conformity at any cost	Procrustes, outlaw who slew strangers
protean	changeable	Proteus, sea god who could change his shape at will
psychology	science of the mind	Psyche, beloved of Cupid
saturnine	gloomy sluggish, grave	Saturn, father of the Olympian gods
tantalize	tease and disappoint	Tantalus, forever condemned to seek food and drink just beyond his reach
titanic	huge	Titans, giants before the Olympic gods
volcano	explosive vent in earth's crust	Vulcan, god of fire
zephyr	gentle breeze	Zephyrus, god of the west wind

INDEX

BIBLIOGRAPHY: ANCIENT PEOPLE II

GREEKS

Armentrout, David and Patricia, *The Treasures from Greece,* The Rourke Book Company, Inc., Vero Beach, FL, 2001.

Boardman, John, *The Oxford History of Classical Art,* Oxford University Press, NY, 1993.

British Museum Press, *The Ancient Greeks Activity Book,* London, 1998.

Chrisp, Peter, *The Parthenon,* Steck-Vaughn Co., Austin, Tx, 1997.

Descamps, Lequine and Denise Verney, *The Ancient Greeks in the Land of the Gods,* Millbrook Press, Brookfield, CT, 1992.

Morgan, Nicola, *People Who Made History in Ancient Greece,* Raintree and Steck, Vaughn Publishers, NY, 2001.

Nardo, Don, *Life in Ancient Athens,* Lucent Books, Inc., San Diego, 2000.

O'Halloran, Kate, *Hands-on Culture of Ancient Greece and Rome,* Walch Publishing, Portland, ME, 1998.

Osborne, Robin, *Archaic and Classical Greek Art,* Oxford University Press, NY, 1998.

Pearson, Anne, *Eyewitness Books: Ancient Greece,* A Dorling Kindersley Book, Alfred A. Knopf, London, 1992.

Pearson, Anne, *Everyday Life in Ancient Greece,* Franklin Watts, NY, 1994.

Schofield, Louise, Ancient Greece, *The Nature Company Discoveries,* Weldon-Owen Inc., Sydney, Austalia, 1997.

Shuter, Jone, *Ancient Greece: Discovery, Invention and Ideas,* Heineman Library, Plaines, IL, 1999.

Shuter, *Ancient Greece: Cities and Citizens,* ibid.

Shuter, *Ancient Greece: Builders, Trades and Craftsmen,* ibid.

Usborne *Encyclopedia of Ancient Greece,* Usborne Publishing Ltd., London, 1999.

ETRUSCANS

Bloch, Raymond, *Etruscan Art,* New York Graphic Society, Greenwich, CT, 1965.

Macnamara, Ellen, *The Etruscans,* Harvard University Press, Cambridge, MA,1991.

Moretti, Mario and Guglielmo Maetzke, *The Art of the Etruscans,* Harry N. Abrams, Inc., NY, 1991.

Sprenger, Maja, Gilda Bartoloni and Albert Hirmer, *The Etruscans,* Harry N. Abrams, Inc., NY, 1983.

Time-Life Books, *The Etruscans: Italy's Lovers of Life,* Alexandria, VA, 1995.

ROMANS

British Museum Press, *The Romans Activity Book,* London, 1999.

Cairns, Trevor, *People Become Civilized: The Cambridge Introduction to History*, Lerner Publications Company, Minneapolis, MN, 1974.

Corbishley, Mike, *The Romans,* Peter Bedrick Books, NY, 1991.

Dineen, Jacqueline, *The Romans,* First New Discovery Books, NY, 1992.

James, Simon, *Ancient Rome,* Doring Kindersley Eyewitness Books, London, 2000.

James, *Ancient Rome with See-Through Scenes,* Viking Penguin, NY, 1992.

Ramage, Nancy and Andrew, *Roman Art: Romulus to Constantine,* Harry N. Abrams, NY, 1991.

Rice, Melanie and Christopher, *Pompeii, The Day a City was Buried,* DK Publishing, NY, 1998.

Seely, John and Elizabeth, *Pompeii and Herculaneum,* Reed Educational and Professional Publishing, Chicago, 2000.

Steele, Philip, *The Romans and Pompeii,* Dillon Press, NY, 1994.

Strong, Donald and David Brown, *Roman Crafts,* New York University Press, 1976.

Hands-on Alaska
(ISBN 0-9643177-3-7)

Hands-on America Vol. I
(ISBN 0-9643177-6-1)

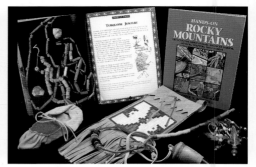

Hands-on Rocky Mountains
(ISBN 0-9643177-2-9)

Hands-on Latin America
(ISBN 0-9643177-1-0)

Hands-on Ancient People - Vol. II
(ISBN 0-9643177-9-6)

Hands-on Celebrations
(ISBN 0-9643177-4-5)

Hands-on Ancient People - Vol. I
(ISBN 0-9643177-8-8)

Hands-on Africa
(ISBN 0-9643177-7-X)

Hands-on Asia
(ISBN 0-9643177-5-3)

Yvonne Merrill's
KITS PUBLISHING

Consider these books for: *the library • teaching social studies • art • ESL programs multicultural programs • museum programs • community youth events • home schooling*

ORDER FORM

SEND TO:_____

ADDRESS:_____

_____

CITY:_____ STATE:_____ ZIP_____

CONTACT NAME: _____ PHONE: _____

PO# _____ FAX: _____

Books are $20⁰⁰ each.

Shipping - $2.00 per book
All books shipped media rate unless otherwise requested.

Make checks payable to:
KITS PUBLISHING • 2359 E. Bryan Avenue • Salt Lake City, Utah 84108
Order by Fax – 801.582.2540
by Phone – 801.582.2517
by email – info@hands-on.com
by the web – www.hands-on.com

❐ ____ **Hands-on Africa**

❐ ____ **Hands-on Alaska**

❐ ____ **Hands-on America Vol I**

❐ ____ **Hands-on Ancient People Vol I**

❐ ____ **Hands-on Ancient People Vol II**

❐ ____ **Hands-on Asia**

❐ ____ **Hands-on Celebrations**

❐ ____ **Hands-on Latin America**

❐ ____ **Hands-on Rocky Mountains**

_____ Total Quantity Ordered

3.00 Handling

_____ Shipping

_____ Total Enclosed/PO